T0338466

GENERALIZED
LR PARSING

GENERALIZED
LR PARSING

edited by

Masaru Tomita
Carnegie Mellon University

Kluwer Academic Publishers
Boston/Dordrecht/London

Distributors for North America:
Kluwer Academic Publishers
101 Philip Drive
Assinippi Park
Norwell, Massachusetts 02061 USA

Distributors for all other countries:
Kluwer Academic Publishers Group
Distribution Centre
Post Office Box 322
3300 AH Dordrecht, THE NETHERLANDS

Consulting Editor: Jaime Carbonell

Library of Congress Cataloging-in-Publication Data

Generalized LR parsing / edited by Masaru Tomita.
    p. cm.
    Includes bibliographical references and index.
    ISBN 0-7923-9201-9
    1. Parsing (Computer grammar) 2. Computational linguistics.
    3. Natural language processing (Computer science) I. Tomita,
Masaru.
  006.3 '5–dc20   91–18965
                                                  CIP

Copyright © 1991 by Kluwer Academic Publishers

All rights reserved. No part of this publication may be reproduced, stored in a retrieval system or transmitted in any form or by any means, mechanical, photo-copying, recording, or otherwise, without the prior written permission of the publisher, Kluwer Academic Publishers, 101 Philip Drive, Assinippi Park, Norwell, Massachusetts 02061.

Printed on acid-free paper.

Printed in the United States of America

Contents

Preface

The Generalized LR parsing algorithm (some call it "Tomita's algorithm") was originally developed in 1985 as a part of my Ph.D thesis at Carnegie Mellon University. When I was a graduate student at CMU, I tried to build a couple of natural language systems based on existing parsing methods. Their parsing speed, however, always bothered me. I sometimes wondered whether it was ever possible to build a natural language parser that could parse reasonably long sentences in a reasonable time without help from large mainframe machines.

At the same time, I was always amazed by the speed of programming language compilers, because they can parse very long sentences (i.e., programs) very quickly even on workstations. There are two reasons. First, programming languages are considerably simpler than natural languages. And secondly, they have very efficient parsing methods, most notably LR. The LR parsing algorithm first precompiles a grammar into an LR parsing table, and at the actual parsing time, it performs shift-reduce parsing guided deterministically by the parsing table. So, the key to the LR efficiency is the grammar precompilation; something that had never been tried for natural languages in 1985.

Of course, there was a good reason why LR had never been applied for natural languages; it was simply impossible. If your context-free grammar is sufficiently more complex than programming languages, its LR parsing table will have multiple actions, and deterministic parsing will be no longer possible. Worst case context-free grammars generate parsing tables that have multiple actions in every entry, and parsing nondeterministically with such a table is as inefficient as parsing without precompilation. Fortunately, typical natural language grammars are not as bad as the worst case grammars. They are very close to LR, and usually only a few entries are multiply defined.

The Generalized LR parsing algorithm handles multiply defined entries gracefully with a device called *graph-structured stack*, preserving most of the LR efficiency. In fact, if the grammar is as simple as a programming language, it behaves exactly like the standard LR parsing algorithm. While its efficiency is still debatable with the unusual worst case grammars, I am confident that the GLR parsing algorithm is clearly more efficient than any other non-precompiling algorithms for practical natural language grammars.

A Common Lisp version of the GLR parser is available for practical natural language projects. It accepts a grammar written in an LFG-like notation. If you are interested in obtaining a copy of the software, contact:

Radha Rao
Center for Machine Translation
Carnegie Mellon University
Pittsburgh, PA 15213, USA
412-268-6591
rdr@nl.cs.cmu.edu

This parser is no longer the only GLR parser. At the first International Workshop on Parsing Technologies (Pittsburgh, 1989), a good number of papers on GLR parsing were presented by many different researchers from all over the world. This book is a collection of selected papers on GLR parsing, most of which were presented at the workshop.

"Chapter 1: The Generalized LR Parsing Algorithm" by me with See-kiong Ng is intended to be a tutorial of the GLR parsing algorithm. This chapter, however, assumes that the reader is familiar with the standard LR parsing algorithm. Those who are not familiar with the standard LR algorithm are suggested to consult [1,2] before reading this chapter. "Chapter 2: Experiments with GLR and Chart Parsing" by Patrick Shann studies practical performance of the GLR parsing algorithm, and comparison with chart parsing is made. "Chapter 3: The Computational Complexity of GLR Parsing" by Mark Johnson analyzes the computational complexity of the GLR parsing algorithm, showing some cases where it takes more than $O(n^3)$ time. "Chapter 4: GLR Parsing in Time $O(n^3)$" by James Kipps presents a modification to the GLR parsing algorithm so that it always runs in time $O(n^3)$. "Chapter 5: GLR-Parsing for ϵ-Grammars" by Rahman Nozohoor-Farshi also modifies the GLR algorithm to handle grammars with empty rules. "Chapter 6: Parallel GLR Parsing Based on Logic Programming" by Hozumi Tanaka and Hiroaki Numazaki describes a parallel implementation of the GLR parsing algorithm in a concurrent logic programming language. "Chapter 7: GLR Parsing with Scoring" by Keh-Yih Su et.al incorporates a scoring mechanism, and "Chapter 8: GLR Parsing with Probability" by J. H. Wright and E. N. Wrigley incorporates probability in the GLR parsing algorithm, respectively, to select the most favorable parse in case of ambiguity. "Chapter 9: GLR Parsing for Erroneous Input" by Stuart Malone and Sue Felshin describes how to handle erroneous input, and "Chapter 10: GLR Parsing for Noizy Input" by Hiroaki Saito and me describes how to handle noisy input with GLR parsing. Both erroneous input and noisy input are ill-formed input, the former being caused by human error and the latter being caused by speech recognition errors. Finally, "Chapter 11: GLR Parsing in Hidden Markov Model" by Kenji Kita et.al describes how the GLR algorithm can be applied to a Hidden Markov Model to constrain search in the speech recognition process.

I wish to thank to Mike Blackwell for his efforts in preparing this manuscript. I also would like to thank to Jaime Carbonell and Herb Simon for their continuous encouragement all the way since I was a first year graduate student more than a decade ago.

References

[1] Aho, A. V. and Ullman, J. D. 1972. *The Theory of Parsing, Translation and Compiling*, Prentice-Hall, Englewood Cliffs, N.J.
[2] Aho, A. V. and Ullman, J. D. 1977. *Principles of Compiler Design*, Addison Wesley.

List of Contributors

Jing-Shin Chang
Institute of Computer Science and Information Engineering,
National Chiao Tung University

Sue Felshin
Athena Language Learning Project, Massachusetts Institute of Technology

Mark Johnson
Brown University

Takeshi Kawabata
ATR Interpreting Telephony Research Laboratories

James R. Kipps
The RAND Corporation

Kenji Kita
ATR Interpreting Telephony Research Laboratories

Stuart Malone
Athena Language Learning Project, Massachusetts Institute of Technology

See-Kiong Ng
School of Computer Science, Carnegie Mellon University

Rahman Nozohoor-Farshi
School of Computer Science, University of Windsor

Hiroaki Numazaki
Tokyo Institute of Technology

Hiroaki Saito
Center for Machine Translation, Carnegie Mellon University
Department of Mathematics, Keio University

Patrick Shann
Office of Automation, Credit Suisse

Keh-Yih Su
Department of Electrical Engineering, National Tsing Hua University

Mei-Hui Su
BTC R&D Center

Hozumi Tanaka
Tokyo Institute of Technology

Masaru Tomita
School of Computer Science, Carnegie Mellon University
Department of Environmental Information, Keio University

Jong-Nae Wang
BTC R&D Center

J. H. Wright
Centre of Communications Research, University of Bristol

E. N. Wrigley
Centre of Communications Research, University of Bristol

GENERALIZED
LR PARSING

1 The Generalized LR Parsing Algorithm

Masaru Tomita and See-Kiong Ng

1.1. Introduction

LR parsing is a widely used method of syntax analysis for a variety of reasons. First and foremost, an LR parser is a deterministic parser which is highly efficient: it scans the input string in one pass and is able to detect errors at an early stage. The availability of parser generators and compiler compilers based on LR parsing technology [2, 4] further accentuated its popularity, since such tools are essential in practical systems where grammars are often too large for a parser to be constructed by hand.

A major drawback of standard LR parsing is that it can only handle a subclass of context-free grammars called *LR grammars*. There are many practical applications, such as in natural language processing, which require more powerful grammatical structures that are not allowed by LR grammars. Although there exist parsing techniques capable of handling arbitrary context-free grammars, for instance, the Earley's algorithm [3] and the Cocke-Younger-Kasami algorithm [5], these algorithms often do not perform as well as LR parsing.

One of the strong points of standard LR parsing is that it is totally deterministic, which gives rise to its efficiency in execution. In order to achieve determinism, the LR parser sacrifices its generality by imposing a stringent condition on the class of grammars over which the technique works. It requires that an LR parsing table with no action conflicts could be generated for the grammar. It is conceivable that in some practical applications, such grammars are hard to come by. For example, in natural language processing, there are grammatical features such as prepositional phrase attachment which are inherently ambiguous, causing any context-free grammar which models the feature to be non-LR. Thus, if there is a general and efficient method for dealing with action conflicts in the parsing table, then there lies an efficient parsing algorithm for general context-free grammar. Generalized LR (GLR) parsing, which was introduced by Tomita in 1985 [7], is one such technology. By using a *graph-structured stack* to simulate nondeterminism, GLR parsers are able to handle general context-free grammars while retaining much of the advantages of standard LR parsing (especially when the grammar is close to being LR). Other deterministic techniques for non-deterministic context-free parsing have been developed independently by Lang [6] and van der Steen [9].

In the following sections, we will first describe the basic notion of the graph-structured stack as a general mechanism. Then, we describe a compacted way of representing the possible parse trees for an ambiguous sentence. Next, to give the reader a fair idea of how a GLR parser actually works, an example trace of the GLR parser on an ambiguous sentence is given. Finally, a specification of the GLR algorithm is presented. In all the discussions, we shall assume that the reader is familiar with the standard LR parsing technique. Extensive descriptions of standard LR parsing can be found in [1, 2].

1.2. Graph-structured Stack

The *graph-structured stack* is a general device for efficient handling of nondeterminism in parsing systems employing a stack. In this section, we shall describe three key notions of the graph-structured stack, namely splitting, combining and local ambiguity packing.

1.2.1. Splitting

When a stack can be reduced (or popped) in more than one way, the top of the stack is made to split to accommodate the various possibilities. Consider the following example. The current stack configuration is displayed below: the stack is represented left to right, that is, the leftmost element A is the bottom of the stack, and the rightmost element E the top of the stack.

$$\boxed{A} - \boxed{B} - \boxed{C} - \boxed{D} - \boxed{E}$$

Now suppose that the stack is to be reduced with each the following three productions in parallel:

$$F \rightarrow D \ E$$
$$G \rightarrow D \ E$$
$$H \rightarrow C \ D \ E$$

After the nondeterministic reduce actions, the stack has the following form:

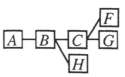

Since the stack has a graph structure, it can have more than one stack top. A stack top in a graph-structured stack, in our left-to-right representation, is a stack node with no nodes attached to its right. In the above example, F, G and H are the stack tops.

1.2.2. Combining

When an element needs to be shifted (pushed) onto more than one stack top, it is done only once by combining the tops of the stack. As a continuation to the previous example, if *I* is to be shifted to *F, G* and *H*, then the resulting stack will look like:

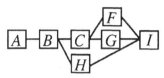

1.2.3. Local Ambiguity Packing

If two or more branches of the stack turn out to be identical, then they represent local ambiguity. That is, the identical state of the stack has been obtained in two or more different ways. These branches are merged and treated as a single branch. To continue from the above example, suppose we are now to reduce the stack by each of the following productions nondeterministically:

$$J \rightarrow F\,I$$
$$J \rightarrow G\,I$$

The resulting stack looks as follows:

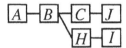

The branch *A–B–C–J* has been obtained in two ways, but they are packed together so that only a single branch remains on the stack.

1.3. Packed Shared Parse Forest

For a highly ambiguous grammar, there might be numerous parse trees generated for the input sentence. Instead of storing each of the parse trees separately, we can exploit the efficient operations of the graph stack to build a *packed shared parse forest* which represents the numerous possible parse trees in a space-efficient manner. To avoid confusion, we shall use the term *vertex* for parse forests, whereas the term *node* refers to an element on the graph-structured stack.

First of all, if two or more trees have a common subtree, the subtree should be represented only once in the parse forest. We call this *subtree sharing* and a parse forest with such property is called a *shared* forest.

We can further minimize the representation of the parse forest by *local ambiguity packing*, which works in the following way. The top vertices of subtrees that represent local ambiguity are merged and treated as if there were only one vertex. We call such a vertex a *packed vertex*. A parse forest with both subtree sharing and local ambiguity packing is called a *packed shared forest*. Figure 1.17 shows a packed shared parse forest for the sentence "*I saw Jane and*

(1)	S	→	NP VP
(2)	S	→	S PP
(3)	S	→	S and S
(4)	NP	→	n
(5)	NP	→	det n
(6)	NP	→	NP PP
(7)	NP	→	NP and NP
(8)	VP	→	v NP
(9)	VP	→	v S
(10)	PP	→	p NP

Figure 1.1. GRA: A non-LR grammar.

Jack hit the man with a telescope," in which the packed vertices are boxed. It is clear from this example that a packed shared parse forest can be represented as a *tree* in which some of the nonterminal vertices (the packed vertices) have possibly several sets of children. Each of the children sets corresponds to a possible derivation of the nonterminal represented by that vertex based on the same input. The numerous parse trees can be easily enumerated from this packed shared parse forest.

It turns out that GLR parsing provides a natural way to construct a packed shared parse forest during parse time. To implement subtree sharing, we push pointers to a vertex of the shared forest together with a stack node. When the parser *shifts* a terminal in the input, it creates a leaf vertex (if it has not already been created) labeled with that terminal and pushes the pointer to this vertex together with the stack node onto the stack. When the parser *reduces* the stack, it pops pointers from the stack, creates a new vertex whose children are the vertices pointed to by these pointers, and pushes the pointer to the new vertex together with the new stack node onto the stack. Packed vertices, on the other hand, are created by the process of *local ambiguity packing* of the graph-structured stack, in which a single stack node is maintained to represent multiple derivations for that nonterminal represented by the node. We can correspondingly append the new set of children vertices for the current derivation to the parse forest vertex in that stack node to create a packed vertex. This process of constructing a packed shared forest with GLR parsing would become clear to the reader with the example in the next section.

1.4. An Example

Figure 1.1 shows a non-LR context-free grammar GRA which contains a fair amount of ambiguity.

GRA is a toy grammar for modeling conjunctive phrases with prepositional attachments in English. Naturally, prepositional attachments and conjunctive grouping are the two main sources of ambiguities here. The former can be exemplified by the sentence "I saw a man with a telescope," for which there are

State	ACTION						GOTO								
	det	n	v	p	and	$	det	n	v	p	and	S	NP	VP	PP
0	sh	sh					2	1				4	3		
1			re4	re4	re4	re4									
2		sh						5							
3			sh	sh	sh				6	7	8			9	10
4				sh	sh	acc				7	11				12
5			re5	re5	re5	re5									
6	sh	sh					2	1				14	13		
7	sh	sh					2	1					15		
8	sh	sh					2	1					16		
9				re1	re1	re1									
10			re6	re6	re6	re6									
11	sh	sh					2	1				17	3		
12				re2	re2	re2									
13			sh	sh,re8	sh,re8	re8			6	7	8			9	10
14				sh,re9	sh,re9	re9				7	11				12
15			re10	sh,re10	sh,re10	re10				7	8				10
16			re7	sh,re7	sh,re7	re7				7	8				10
17				sh,re3	sh,re3	re3				7	11				12

Figure 1.2. SLR(1) parsing table for GRA.

two different interpretations due to ambiguous prepositional attachment:

1. [I saw [a man with a telescope]]
2. [I saw [a man] with a telescope]

Ambiguity due to conjunctive grouping can be illustrated by the sentence "I know Jane and Jack knew it":

1. I know [Jane and Jack knew it].
2. [I know Jane] and [Jack knew it].

The interaction between these two sources of ambiguities worsens the situation, such as in the sentence "I saw Jane and Jack hit the man with a telescope." Sometimes, such ambiguities can be resolved by using punctuations in the text (for example, by inserting a comma at the boundaries of conjunctive groupings), intonation in speech, or semantic and contextual information. The problem is that such additional information may not be available at parse time. The parser is often obliged to generate all syntactically consistent interpretations until further information can be used for disambiguation.

1.4.1. A Sample Parse with GLR

Figure 1.2 shows an SLR(1) parsing table for GRA as constructed using the simple-LR table construction method described in [1, 2].

The parsing table consists of two parts: an ACTION table and a GOTO table. The ACTION table is indexed by a state symbol *s* (row) and a terminal

symbol x (column), including the end marker \$. The entry ACTION$[s, x]$ can
be one of the following: *sh, re n, acc* or blank. *sh* denotes a shift action, *re n*
means a reduction by the n-th production, *acc* denotes the accept action and a
blank indicates a parsing error. The GOTO table is indexed by a state symbol s
(row) and a grammar symbol X (column). The entry GOTO$[s, X]$ defines the
next state the parser should go to. During parse time, the parser consults the
ACTION table for parsing actions to execute based on its current configuration,
executes the actions accordingly, and then refers to the GOTO table for its next
state.

In the following, we give a trace of the GLR algorithm on the input sentence
"I saw Jane and Jack hit the man with a telescope." In each step of the trace,
we show the following:

- *The graph-structured stack:* Each stack node is represented either as a square or a
  circle with a state number in it and the corresponding parse forest vertex above it.
  An active top node is depicted as a circle, with the pending parsing actions placed
  next to it. Although we do not actually delete the stack nodes during reduction, we
  have chosen not to display the irrelevant nodes in our trace diagrams for the sake of
  clarity.
- *The packed shared parse forest:* Each vertex in the parse forest is labeled as X_n,
  where X is a grammar symbol represented by that vertex, and n is a unique subscript
  which distinguishes vertices in the forest that represent the same grammar symbol.
  An ordinary vertex is represented as a dot, whereas a packed vertex is represented
  as a highlighted box encompassing the dots (vertices) that represent the various
  possible parses for the locally ambiguous symbol. On the parse stack, a star is
  placed momentarily beside the respective parse vertex to indicate where and when
  local ambiguity packing has occurred.
- *Next input word:* We indicate the next word on the input sentence at the top of each
  trace diagram. It is shown as a pair $"w" {:} x$, where w is the actual form of the word in
  the input sentence, and x a terminal symbol in the grammar which corresponds to the
  lexical category of w. We assume that every word can be categorized unambiguously,
  although the parser could easily handle lexical ambiguities by treating the various
  possibilities as action conflicts [7].
- *Next ACTIONs and GOTO states:* The parsing actions, which are placed beside the
  respective active top nodes, are specified as pairs $[a, s]$, where a is the ACTION to
  be performed on the node, and s is the corresponding GOTO state after executing
  a. Let us call a node that immediately precedes a reduction path on the stack a *base*
  node. For a reduction which splits a merged node, each of the base nodes' goto
  states are represented in a column in the top-down order in which the base nodes are
  depicted in the graph.

We are now ready to begin the trace of the GLR parser on the sentence:
"I saw Jane and Jack hit the man with a telescope."
Initially, the stack contains only one node with state 0, and the parse forest is
null (represented as $\perp$). The next word is "I," which is categorized as a noun n.
Since ACTION$[0, n] = sh$ and GOTO$[0, n] = 1$, we place the pair $[sh, 1]$ next
to the node, which is denoted by a circle since it is currently an active stack top
(see Figure 1.3).

Next word = "I" : n

Figure 1.3. Trace of the parser.

Next word = "saw" : v

Figure 1.4. Trace of the parser (cont'd).

Next word = "Jane" : n

Figure 1.5. Trace of the parser (cont'd).

In executing the shift action, the parser creates a parse forest vertex n_1 for the word "I," and pushes a stack node of state 1 and vertex n_1 onto the stack. The next word is "saw," which is a verb v. Since $ACTION[1, v] = re4$ and $GOTO[0, NP] = 3$ (as production 4 is $NP \rightarrow n$ and the base node for this reduction is the start node, which has state 0), this new node is active with the pair $[re4, 3]$, as shown in the first row of Figure 1.4. The second row shows the resulting configuration of the parser after this reduce action is executed: a new parse forest vertex NP_1 whose child is n_1 is created, the stack nodes along the reduction paths are popped, and a new node with state 3 and vertex NP_1 is pushed onto the stack. The action-goto pair for this new active stack top is $[sh, 6]$.

After the shift action for the word "saw" is executed, the resulting configuration calls for another shift action for the input "Jane," as depicted in Figure 1.5.

After the word "Jane" is shifted onto the stack, the next word is the conjunction "and." The first action to execute is "*re 4*" (see the first row of Figure 1.6). This reduction results in a new stack node of state 13 and parse forest vertex NP_2, as shown in the second row of the figure. At this node, the parser encounters, for the first time, a parsing action conflict, since $ACTION[13, and]$ can be "*sh*" or "*re 8*." Since the GLR algorithm requires that

Next word = "and" : and

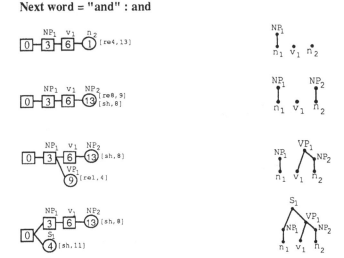

Figure 1.6. Trace of the parser (cont'd).

Next word = "Jack" : n

Figure 1.7. Trace of the parser (cont'd).

all the current reduce actions be processed before the shifts, the parser leaves this top node active with the shift action for now. The *"re 8"* action is executed, creating a new branch on the stack (see the third row of the figure). A further reduction of the new branch occurs, after which both branches of the stack are left with pending shift actions, as in the last row of the figure.

The two shift actions for the word "and" are then executed, and Figure 1.7 shows the resulting configuration of the parser. The next word is "Jack," which is a noun n. This time, both of the stack tops are active with the same shift-goto pair $[sh, 1]$. This calls for a *combining* of shift nodes on the stack, so the parser generates a single merged node for both shifts. The outcome is depicted in the first row of Figure 1.8 where the next word to be parsed is "hit."

In parsing the word "hit," another instance of graph-stack splitting occurs (see rows 1 and 2 of Figure 1.8). In this case, the parser begins with a merged stack top which is active with a *"re 4"* action. Since there are two base nodes (namely, the nodes with states 8 and 11) with different goto states (GOTO[8,NP]=16 and GOTO[11, NP]=3), the popping of the merged node results in a pair of stack tops. As there is only one reduction path, a single parse vertex NP_3 is created.

Next word = "hit" : v

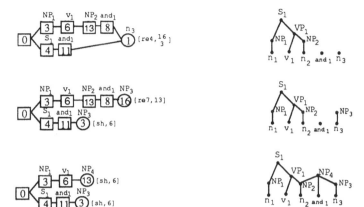

Figure 1.8. Trace of the parser (cont'd).

Next word = "the" : det

Figure 1.9. Trace of the parser (cont'd).

Next word = "man" : n

Figure 1.10. Trace of the parser (cont'd).

Two new stack nodes with states 16 and 3, both sharing NP_3 as their parse forest vertex, are pushed onto the respective base nodes. One of the stack tops (the one with state 16) is active with a reduce action, while the other (the one with state 3) a shift action. Following the policy of GLR, we process the reduce action first. The outcome of this reduction is depicted in the last row of Figure 1.8, where both of the top nodes are active with the same shift-goto pair.

Figure 1.9 shows the result of pushing a combined node onto the stack for the word "hit." The next word is the determiner "the," which calls for a shift action.

Figure 1.10 shows the configuration of the parser after "the" is shifted onto the stack. The action with the next word "man" is again a shift.

Next word = "with":p

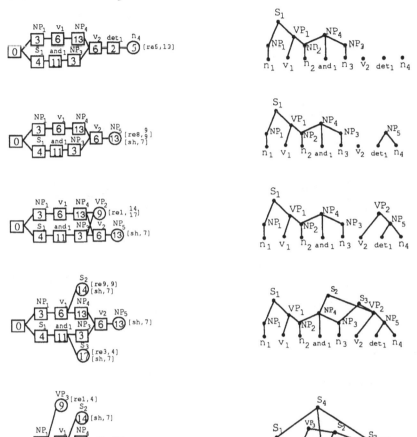

Figure 1.11. Trace of the parser (cont'd).

In Figures 1.11 and 1.12, the execution sequence of the parser in parsing the preposition "with" is shown.

Let us pay particular attention to the last row of Figure 1.11, especially the active top node with state 9, of which the pending action-goto pair is $[re1, 4]$. The only base node for this reduction is the bottom stack node. However, this base node already has a child node of state 4 which was also created for the current input (from the execution of $[re3, 4]$ on the top node with state 17 in the previous row). This indicates that the current input ("I saw Jane and Jack hit the man") can be reduced into an S in more than one way. Thus, the parser performs

Next word = "with" : p (cont'd)

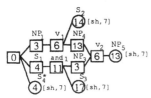
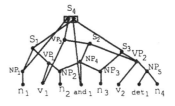

Figure 1.12. Trace of the parser (cont'd).

Next word = "a": det

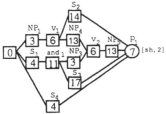
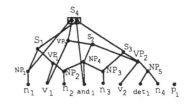

Figure 1.13. Trace of the parser (cont'd).

local ambiguity packing as follows. Instead of creating another stack node and parse forest vertex for the current reduction, the parser packs the new reduction into the parse vertex S_4, causing it to have two sets of children vertices, each corresponding to a possible derivation of S from the input "I saw Jane and Jack hit the man" (which can be interpreted as either "[I saw Jane] and [Jack hit the man]," or "I saw [Jane and Jack hit the man]"). Since this stack node has been created previously by another reduction of the current input, it must be the case that further parsing actions on this node are already taken care of. Thus, the parser does not have to pursue further after packing the parse forest vertex S_3 in this node. Figure 1.12 shows the resulting packed shared parse forest. We indicate where local ambiguity packing occurs on the graph-structured stack by a starred parse vertex (S_4^*). Also, in Figure 1.12, all the four active stack tops are left with the same shift-goto pair. Again, a combined node for the preposition "with" is created and pushed onto the four tops, the result of which can be seen in Figure 1.13.

Figure 1.13 and 1.14 show the parsing of the last two words in the input sentence, "a" and "telescope," respectively. In each case, a shift action is called to push the word onto the stack.

At this point, the parser has reached the end of the input sentence, so the READ head is looking the end marker "$." Figures 1.15 and 1.16 shows the sequence of actions taken by the parser towards a final *"accept"* action. The

Next word = "telescope": n

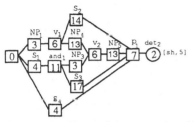
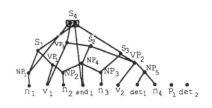

Figure 1.14. Trace of the parser (cont'd).

Next word = "$" : $

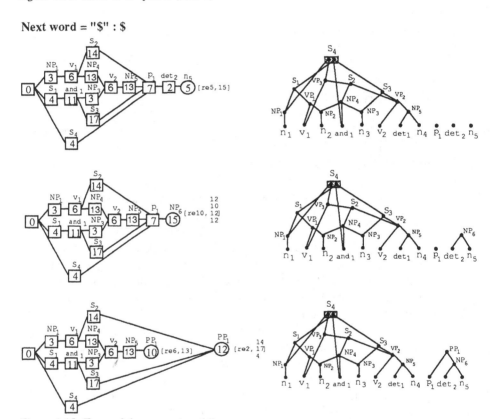

Figure 1.15. Trace of the parser (cont'd).

final configuration of the parser is one in which there is only a single active top node on the graph-structured stack, whose only pending action is an *"accept"* action (see the last row of Figure 1.16). The parser thus halts in an accepting state.

The final parse forest (and the 6 possible parse trees) is shown in Figure 1.17.

Next word = "$": $ (cont'd)

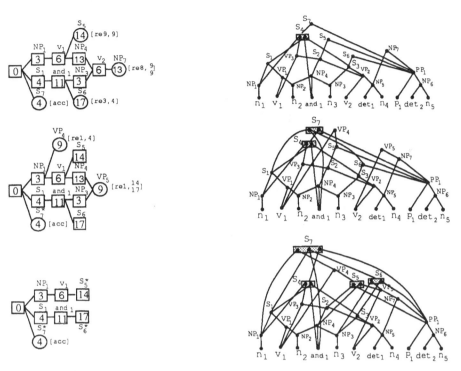

Figure 1.16. Trace of the parser (cont'd).

1.5. Specification of the GLR Parsing Algorithm

The following is a specification of the GLR(k) parsing algorithm for context-free grammars without ϵ-productions. The algorithm can be easily modified to handle ϵ-productions (see Chapter 5).

The k in this specification refers to the number of input symbols the parser looks ahead during parse time in determining what parsing actions to execute. Thus, the ACTION table is indexed by a state and a lookahead string of k terminal symbols, including end-markers $'s. The GOTO table is indexed by a state and a single grammar symbol. Usually, longer lookaheads are employed during parsing table construction to avoid action conflicts [1, 2] so that standard LR parsing can be applied. However, longer lookaheads also result in larger parsing tables. Since generalized LR can handle multiple entries, the choice of k in GLR parsing would depend on the tradeoff between the size of the parsing table and the efficiency obtained from the extra degree of determinism due to longer lookaheads. In our previous example, we used a single lookahead, that is, $k = 1$.

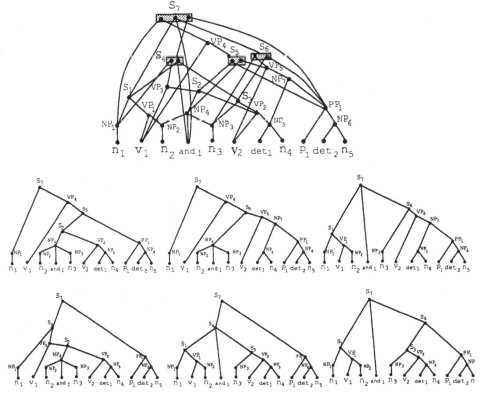

Figure 1.17. Packed shared forest and its respective parse trees.

Algorithm 1.1 *GLR(k) Parsing Algorithm*

Input: A parsing table for a grammar $G = (N, \Sigma, P, S)$ in terms of an ACTION
   table which may contain multiple entries, a GOTO function, and an input
   string $z \in \Sigma^*$. N is the set of nonterminals for G, Σ is the set of terminals,
   P is the set of productions, and $S \in N$ is the start symbol. The ACTION
   table uses a lookahead string of length k. The state s_0 is designated as
   the initial state.

Output: If $z \in L(G)$, the root vertex of a packed shared parse forest for z.
   Otherwise, an error indication.

Method: Patch the input string z with k end markers, giving the string $z\$^k$.
   Make a stack node η_0 containing the start state s_0. η_0 forms the bottom
   of the parse stack. Other than η_0, a stack node normally contains two
   fields: the state of the parser and the corresponding parse forest vertex.
   Initially, the READ head is pointing at the first symbol of z. Let u denote
   the lookahead string, which consists of the next k input symbols from
   the READ head. For each non-error action $a \in \text{ACTION}[s_0, u]$, add the

pair (η_0, a) to an associative list called FRONTIER. The nodes found in the node-action pairs in FRONTIER are the active stack tops. Repeatedly perform step 1, 2, 3 and 4 (in this order) until an acceptance or rejection occurs.

1. Remove an element of the form $(\eta, \textit{reduce } A \rightarrow \alpha)$ from FRONTIER. Collect P, the set of paths of length $|\alpha|$ ending at η (a path is a contiguous sequence of nodes on the graph). For each path $p \in P$, we create a new parse vertex ν_p to be used in the parse forest as the parent vertex for that reduction. Also, for each p, collect the set of stack nodes which immediately precedes p. We call these nodes the *base nodes* for p, and denote the set as B_p. Partition B_p according to their next goto states. Let $b_s \subseteq B_p$ be the set of nodes in B_p such that s is the GOTO state of every node in b_s on seeing the grammar symbol A.

   For each set b_s in the partition, check if there is a node η' on the stack which has been created with the current input, whose children set is the set b_s, and whose parse vertex represents the nonterminal A (and consequently, its state is also s). If so, then local ambiguity has occurred and we can re-use the node η' as the stack node for the current reduction. We pack the parse forest vertex in η' by adding to its children set the corresponding vertex path in p. Otherwise, we create a new stack node η'' with s as its state and ν_p as its parse vertex, and make ν_p's children set contain the corresponding vertex path in p. Push η'' onto the stack nodes in b_s, and update the FRONTIER by adding to it a pair (η'', a) for each non-error action $a \in \text{ACTION}[s, u]$.

   Repeat Step 1 until none of the stack tops are active with a reduce action.

2. Remove all pairs from FRONTIER of the form $(\eta, \textit{shift})$. Let the stack nodes in these pairs be $\eta_1, \ldots, \eta_m$, whose states are $s_1, \ldots, s_m$ respectively. Create a new parse vertex ν for u_1, the first symbol in u. Advance the READ head one symbol to the right and let the new lookahead string be w. Let Π be the partition of $\eta_1, \ldots, \eta_m$ according to their next GOTO states. That is, if $\text{GOTO}[s_i, u_1] = \text{GOTO}[s_j, u_1] = s$ for some state s, then η_i and η_j belongs to the same set π_s in Π.

   For each $\pi_s \in \Pi$, create a single stack node η_s with state s and parse forest vertex ν, and push η_s onto the stack nodes in π_s. Add to FRONTIER a pair (η_s, a) for each non-error action $a \in \text{ACTION}[s, w]$.

3. If FRONTIER $= \big\{(\eta, accept)\big\}$, we accept and return the parse vertex in η.

4. If FRONTIER $= \emptyset$, we halt and reject.

1.6. Concluding Remarks

In this chapter, we saw how standard LR parsing evolves into GLR parsing which handles general context-free grammars instead of LR grammars while retaining much of the efficiency of standard LR parsing. The graph-structured stack and the shared packed parse forest made the efficiency of LR parsing available to natural language processing. Subsequent chapters by different contributors shall discuss empirical and theoretical performances of GLR parsing, as well as its application to ill-formed input, probabilistic grammars and speech recognition.

References

[1] Aho, A.V. and Ullman, J.D. 1972. *The Theory of Parsing, Translation, and Compiling Vol 1: Parsing*, Prentice-Hall, Englewood Cliffs, New Jersey.

[2] Aho, A.V. and Ullman, J.D. 1977. *Principles of Compiler Design*, Addison Wesley.

[3] Earley, J. 1970. *An Efficient Context-free Parsing Algorithm*, ACM Communications, 13(2):94-102.

[4] Johnson, S.C. 1975. *YACC — Yet Another Compiler Compiler*, CSTR 32, Bell Laboratories, Murray Hill, N.J.

[5] Kasami, T. 1965. *An Efficient Recognition and Syntax Analysis Algorithm for Context-free Languages*, Sci. Rep. AFCRL-65-758, Air Force Cambridge Research Laboratory, Bedford, MA.

[6] Lang, B. 1974. *Deterministic Techniques for Efficient Non-deterministic Parsers*, Proceedings of 2nd Colloquium on Automata, Languages and Programming, Jacques Loeckx (Ed). Lecture Notes in Computer Science (14), edited by G. Goos and J. Hartmanis, Springer-Verlag Berlin.

[7] Tomita, M. 1985. *Efficient Parsing for Natural Language*, Kluwer Academic Publishers, Boston, MA.

[8] Tomita, M. January-June, 1987. An Efficient Augmented Context-Free Parsing Algorithm, *Computational Linguistics* 13(1-2):31-46.

[9] Van der Steen, G.J. 1987. *A Program Generator for Recognition, Parsing and Transduction with Syntactic Patterns*, vakgroep Alfa-informatica, Faculteit der Letteren, Universiteit van Amsterdam

2 Experiments with GLR and Chart Parsing

Patrick Shann

2.1. Introduction

The chapter reports the results of a practical comparison of different parsing strategies. The research was carried out in the context of a larger project for the development of a machine translation (MT) system for translating avalanche forecast bulletins from German to French. The design of the MT system requires controlled input and no post-editing of the translated texts. The parsing experiment had as a goal to select the most suitable parsing strategy for a parser that allows the composition of the sentences in on-line fashion with mouse and windowing.[1] In order to guarantee correct translation, the input system accepts only words and sentences that are known by their grammar and dictionary and it refuses wrong input. To minimize input errors, the user can select the possible next words with the mouse from different windows, which display the choices at a particular point in the sentence. The sentences are parsed word by word from left to right so that wrong input is detected immediately. After each word, the input device has to predict, with the help of the parser, all the words that can possibly continue the sentence that is being made. For our type of on-line parser, time is critical. The interface window has to be refreshed immediately after each word chosen by the user.

When we looked for a suitable parser, no comparison existed between Tomita's extended LR parser and enhanced chart parsers (top-down filter, rule compiling and selectivity) using different strategies (CKY, LC, BI[2]) apart from Tomita's own comparison with the Earley parser (TD). Furthermore, practical tests (Wirén 1987) are normally performed by using only simple phrase structure grammars and by measuring pure parse time. In our experiment we were interested in real time performance (what is seen by a user). Since the grammar type can heavily influence the overall processing efficiency, we chose to base our experience on three grammar types in the paradigm of context-free parsing (monadic, simple features and unification). Our parsing experiment is a continuation of the work of J. Slocum (1981a) and M. Tomita (1985) on parsing algorithms and parsing strategies. The emphasis of the research lies on the real-world performance of the parsers in connection with different

---

1. A system with a similar input facility is reported by H. R. Tennant (1983).
2. S. Steel and A. De Roeck (1987).

grammar types rather than on the theoretical space and time complexity of the parsers.

2.2. Description of the Parsers

In our experiment, we have compared the Tomita parser with four chart-parsers[3] that have different rule-invocation strategies. In this section we will introduce the different parsing strategies and the improvements that can be made, i.e. top-down filtering, selectivity and rule compilation.

2.2.1. Chart Parsers

Our four chart parsers can be distinguished in the way they define the two basic operations Combine and Propose.[4] Combine is the procedure that builds new edges in the chart by combining existing ones, Propose is the rule invocation strategy that predicts new edges on the basis of the grammar. In the next chapter we define the basic algorithms. The improvements of the chart parsers are described in the following chapters on top-down filtering, selectivity and rule compilation.

2.2.1.1. Four different chart parsers: TD, LC, CKY, BI.   Let G be a context-free grammar with S as start symbol. We will represent terminal symbols by lowercase letters: a, b, c; nonterminals by capitals: A, B, C; strings of terminals or nonterminals with Greek letters: α, β, γ; vertices by: i, j, k; edges[5] as pairs of the rule in dotted notation and their left and right vertices. We will call the first symbol to the right of the dot in an active edge the required category. In the following example of an active edge, $\langle A \rightarrow B \cdot CD | i, j \rangle$, C is the required category, i the left and j the right vertex. TD, LC are implemented in such a way that they use only active edges, CKY only complete edges and BI active and complete edges.

Top-down (TD).   This strategy can be considered as Earley-like since it is very similar to Earley's algorithm apart from the fact that it does not use a lookahead. Some authors describe its Combine as the "fundamental rule" of chart parsing.[6]

3. We assume basic familiarity with chart parsing and with Tomita's LR parsing algorithm. For further literature on charts see Wirén (1987), for LR parsing Aho & Ullman (1979).
4. Our Combine is more general than Winograds (1983) since we use a CKY variant with complete edges only.
5. Edges correspond to Earley's (1970) "states" and to "items" in Aho & Ullman (1977).
6. H. Thompson (1981). We will describe the two operations in a similar style to Thompson and Wirén (1987).

Combine
Whenever a complete edge $E_c\langle A \rightarrow \alpha \cdot |j,k\rangle$ is added to the chart, combine it with all active edges $E_a\langle B \rightarrow \beta \cdot C\gamma|i,j\rangle$ ending at E_c's starting point j if E_c's category A corresponds to E_a's required category C and build the corresponding new edges $\langle B \rightarrow \beta C \cdot \gamma|i,k\rangle$.

Propose
Whenever an active edge $E_a\langle A \rightarrow \alpha \cdot B\beta|i,j\rangle$ is added to the chart, if its required category B is a nonterminal, for every rule $B \rightarrow \gamma$ in the grammar G that expands E_a's required category B add an empty edge $E_x\langle B \rightarrow \cdot\gamma|j,j\rangle$.

The parse runs top-down and is triggered by the first active edge $\langle S \rightarrow \cdot\alpha|0,0\rangle$ expanding a with all the rules that have the start symbol S as left-hand side. It proceeds in a strict left-to-right fashion, the next input word is read when all Proposes and Combines up to the current input point have been executed. Opposed to the TD strategy are the two typical bottom-up parsers LC and CKY. Instead of using the rule selecting mechanism for building new hypotheses or active edges on the basis of required categories, the bottom-up parsers trigger the rules from the categories of complete edges.

Left-corner (LC).   As a bottom-up technique new edges are proposed on the basis of complete edges. The corresponding grammar rules are triggered if the first symbol of the right-hand side (RHS) of the rule, the "left- corner," has the same category as the complete edge. LC and TD have the same "Combine" and expand active edges from left to right.

Propose
Whenever a complete edge $E_a\langle A \rightarrow \alpha \cdot |i,j\rangle$ is added to the chart, for every rule $B \rightarrow A\beta$ in the grammar G whose left-corner symbol A has the same category as E_a, add an active edge $E_n\langle B \rightarrow A \cdot \beta|i,j\rangle$ to the chart.

Cocke-Kasami-Younger (CKY).   The second bottom-up parser is a variant of the Cock-Kasami-Younger algorithm. It is similar to CKY in the sense that it is pure bottom-up and combines only complete edges, but the grammar rules are not restricted to Chomsky normal form. To achieve this, Combine works from the right to the left and the rules are proposed on the rightmost symbol of the right-hand side. Propose does not build active edges as in the two previous chart parsers but it is in this context a subfunction that guides Combine by proposing all possible rules for combining complete edges.

Propose
Whenever a complete edge $E_c\langle A \rightarrow \alpha \cdot |i,j\rangle$ is added to the chart, propose all rules $B \rightarrow \beta A$ in the grammar G, whose rightmost symbol is A.

Combine
Whenever a complete edge $E_c\langle A \rightarrow \alpha \cdot |i,j\rangle$ is added to the chart, for each rule $B \rightarrow \beta A$ that is proposed on A and for each combination of consecutive[7] complete

---

7. Two complete edges can be combined to the left if the starting vertex of the first edge corresponds

edges starting with E_c and going to the left whose categories satisfy the sequence bA build a new complete edge $E_n \langle B \rightarrow \beta A \cdot | k, j \rangle$ starting at the vertex k of its left-most edge and ending at the right vertex j of E_c.

Bi-directional (BI).   De Roeck (1987) gives the following motivation for bi-directional rule invocation. Form a linguistic point of view, certain phenomena like traces are best analysed top-down whereas others are best discovered from evidence in the string, e.g. in coordination, the conjunction is the best evidence for triggering the rule. But in the two bottom-up chart parsers the rules are triggered by a fixed handle, which is either the left-most or the right-most symbol of the RHS of a rule. In bi-directional chart parsing the linguist can tailor the rule invoking strategy locally by annotating the rules if they are used top-down or bottom-up. For bottom-up rules, one has to indicate which symbol they are triggered on. A rule for coordinating N_p's can be annotated for example "up" on the conjunction: $N_p \rightarrow N_p \mathrm{Conj} N_p \{\mathrm{upConj}\}$. When the complete edge for Conj is added to the chart, this rule will be triggered and it will add an active edge that tries to combine with an NP to the left as well as to the right. The Propose of the bi-directional parser acts according the the annotation of the rules. In order to avoid duplication Combine has been implemented in such a way that it first combines to the left and only then to the right. We have to expand the dotted rule notation in the sense that a colon marks the beginning of the recognized symbols of an edge and the dot the end of the recognized parts. Symbols to the right of a colon and to the left of a dot have been recognized. Our implementation proposes only to the right. An active edge can be left-active, if it is expecting a symbol to the left.

Propose
Whenever a complete edge $E_a \langle A \rightarrow: \gamma \cdot | i, j \rangle$ is added to the chart, for every rule $B \rightarrow \alpha A \beta$ annotated bottom-up on the symbol A, add an active edge $E_n \langle B \rightarrow \alpha : A \cdot \beta | i, j \rangle$ to the chart.

Whenever an active edge $E_a \langle A \rightarrow: \alpha \cdot B\beta | i, j \rangle$ is added to the chart, if its required category B is a nonterminal, add an empty active edge $E_x \langle B \rightarrow \cdot \delta | j, j \rangle$ for each rule in the grammar G that is annotated down and that expands E_a's required category B.

Combine
Whenever a left active edge $E_a \langle A \rightarrow \alpha : \gamma \cdot \beta | i, j \rangle$ is added to the chart, for each combination of complete edges starting with E_a and going to the left whose categories satisfy the sequence a build a new active edge $E_n \langle A \rightarrow: \alpha\gamma \cdot \beta | k, j \rangle$ starting at the vertex k of its left-most edge and ending at the right vertex j of E_a.

Whenever a complete edge $E_c \langle A \rightarrow \alpha \cdot | j, k \rangle$ is added to the chart, combine it with all active edges $E_a \langle B \rightarrow: \beta \cdot C\gamma | i, j \rangle$ ending at E_c's starting point j if E_c's category A corresponds to E_a's required category C and build the corresponding new edges $\langle B \rightarrow: \beta C \cdot \gamma | i, k \rangle$.

---

to the ending vertex of the second one.

The bi-directional chart parser was included in the tests for verifying the hypothesis if triggering annotations of the rules reduce the search space and improve the overall performance.

2.2.1.2. Top-down filter (Tdf).   In general, bottom-up algorithms reduce the search space by the fact that they are data-driven. On evidence of complete edges, that are present in the string, they are faster in finding the corresponding rules. They do not have to explore the whole search space of the grammar as the TD parser that is over-productive in active edges. On the other hand, bottom-up parsers have problems in dealing with rules that have common right parts as in the following example: CD is the common right string of both rules $A \rightarrow BCD$ and $A \rightarrow CD$. Both rules will fire on a string BCD. Bottom-up chart parsers are over-productive in complete edges that do not attach to phrases on the left. The next two chapters deal with filters to reduce over-production of useless edges: top-down-filtering, a method for bottom-up parsers to reduce the production of useless complete edges and selectivity, a method to reduce the production of unnecessary active edges, useful for TD, LC and BI.

Top-down-filtering is described like running a top-down parser in parallel with a bottom-up parser.[8] The bottom-up parser proposes new edges while the top-down process checks if they can be derived from the root. The Tdf rejects all proposed rules that will generate phrases that can't be attached to the left context. The Tdf uses a "reachability relation R where $A R B$ holds if there exists some derivation from A to B such that B is the left-most element in a string derived from A" (Wirén 1987, cf also Pratt 1975). The reachability relation R can be precompiled so that the Tdf can check in constant time if R holds for a new proposed edge.

In the LC parser, the Tdf is implemented in the following way: For each nonterminal category A the transitive closure of the relation R of the categories that are reachable from A are precalculated . At each vertex, the Tdf keeps a list of the reachable categories. Vertex 0 is initialised with the list of the categories that are reachable from the root category. For each new active edge E_n, the Tdf adds the categories that are reachable from the new required category to the Tdf-list of reachable categories at the ending vertex of E_n. In the function Propose, the Tdf checks for every proposed rule if its left-hand side category is in the list of the reachable categories of the current vertex. Only rules that pass the Tdf lead to the creation of new active edges.

2.2.1.3. Lookahead (La) and selectivity (Sel).   Top-down-filtering cuts down the production of useless complete edges in bottom-up parsing by checking if they can combine with the left context. The lookahead function verifies if a

---

8. J. Slocum (1981b), M. Kay (1982), Pratt (1975), Wirén (1987).

new edge can be attached to the right context. This function is used by Earley's algorithm. Wirén (1987) reports an experiment where selectivity (Sel) was used successfully to reduce the over-production of active edges in TD or LC.[9] Sel is based on the same reachability relation R as Tdf but it is looking to the right as La. Each time an active edge is proposed, the Sel function checks if the new required category C_n can reach the preterminal category of the next input word a_{i+1}, that is if $C_n R a_{i+1}$ holds. We have concentrated our tests on the selectivity function without considering lookaheads.

2.2.1.4. Rule compilation.   The third method for reducing the number of edges in chart parsing is precompiling the grammar rules into decision trees. Assume two rules used by a LC parser, $A \to BC$ and $A \to BDE$. The two rules have the common left part B and can therefore be merged into a single combined rule with a shared part B: $A \to B(C, DE)$. In parsing, the two rules can share the common part B which is represented by a single active edge. TD and LC compile the rules by factoring out similar left parts. CKY combines from right to left and does therefore the factoring from the right. BI, based on annotations of single rules, uses both ways of building its rule decision trees. Note that building decision trees for rules is related to the way in which the canonical set of items is built for the construction of LR parsing tables. The first step in making a new canonical LR set is done by taking all the items in a set that have the same category to the right of the dot. Building decision trees from rules also groups them together on the basis of the next category that has to be recognized.

2.2.2. Tomita's Extended LR Parser (TOM)

Tomita's Parser (Tomita 1985) is a generalised version of a LR shift-reduce parser. It is based on two data structures: a graph structured stack and a parser forest for representing the result. The graph-structured stack allows nondeterministic parsing of ambiguous grammars with LR shift-reduce technique. Tomita (1988) shows that his graph-structured stack is very similar to the chart in chart parsing. The parse forest allows an efficient representation of the result. While the number of parses can grow exponentially, the parse forest grows polynomially. In order to see which part of the program is responsible for efficiency, we compare two versions of Tomita's parser, one with and one without parse forest.

2.2.3. The Grammar Types

Each parser can be run with three different types of context-free grammars. This

---

9. Earley uses the lookahead in a different way: The lookahead is in his Completer and not in the Predictor, as in Wiréns programms.

is done by adding annotations to the context-free rule skeleton. Whenever all constituents of a context-free rule are found, before the new edge is constructed, the parser calls for a rule-body procedure (Slocum 1981b) that evaluates the annotations of the rule. Each grammar type has a different module for evaluating the rule-body procedure. If the rule-body procedure returns an error because a test has failed, the new edge is discarded.

The first grammar type uses simple phrase structure rules with monadic categories that have no annotations. The second grammar type has annotations that go with simple sets of attribute-value pairs where the values are atomic. These annotations allow testing and assigning features to particular nodes of the context-free rules. The third grammar type is unification based and uses complex features and annotations in the PATR-II style. The three grammar types vary the rule-body procedure overhead (unification being very time consuming) and therefore show a more realistic picture of the behaviour of the parsers in real context.

2.3. Previous Empirical Comparisons

In this section we report the results of three practical comparisons of parsers relevant to our experiment: Slocum who compared particularly LC and CKY with top-down filter, Tomita who compared his extended LR parser with Earley's parser and Wirén who compared TD and LC with top-down filter and selectivity. Each of the comparisons gives an incomplete picture. They usually compare two basic strategies with different refinements like top-down filtering etc.

One of the important points for comparisons is stressed by Slocum (1981b): Theoretical calculations about worst case behaviour of algorithms can be quite inaccurate because they often neglect the constant factors that seem to have a dominant effect in practical situations. He writes: "In order to meaningfully describe performance, one must take into account the complete operational context of the natural language processing system, particularly the expenses encountered in storage management and applying rule-body procedures" since a significant portion of the sentence analysis effort may be invested in evaluating the rule-body procedures. To measure performance accurately he suggests including "everything one actually pays for in real computing world: Paging, storage management, building interpretations, rule-body procedure, etc., as well as parse time."

2.3.1. Slocum: Two Bottom-up Chart Parsers, LC vs. CKY

Slocum has conducted two experiments, one at SRI and the second one at LRC, which is more important for us. In the second experiment, he carefully compared two bottom-up chart parsers: LC and CKY enhanced with top-down filtering and early constituent tests.[10] He used the German analysis grammar ($\sim$ 500 rules) of the MT system that was under development at the time at LRC and a corpus of 262 sentences going from 1 – 39 words per sentence (15.6 words/sentence average). The rule-body procedures were rather considerable for a parser test but interesting for realistic performance evaluation. They consisted of "the complete analysis procedures for the purpose of subsequent translation which includes the production of a full syntactic and semantic analysis via phrase- structure rules, feature tests and operations, transformations and case frames."

Given his grammar and test sentences Slocum establishes two things:

1. LC with Tdf (without early constituent test) performs best, better than CKY (which is the opposite of the common expectation). He comments that a Tdf increases the search space, but that the overhead is balanced in practice by the fact that the Tdf reduces the number of phrases and therefore particularly the rule-body procedure overhead, which is considerable in his case. "The overhead for filtering in LC is less than that in CKY. This situation is due to the fact that LC maintains a natural left-right ordering of the rule constituents in its internal representation, whereas CKY does not and must therefore compute it at run time."
2. "The benefits of top-down filtering are dependent on sentence length: in fact filtering is detrimental for shorter sentences. Averaging over all other strategies, the break-even point for top- down filtering occurs at about 7 words."

We conclude this section with a statement from Slocum about filters: "Filtering always increases pure parse time because the parser sees it as pure overhead. The benefits are only observable in overall system performance, due primarily to a significant reduction in the time/space spent evaluating rule-body procedures." This point will be important in our comparisons since we use three different grammar types with rule-body procedures that take increasingly more time.

2.3.2. Tomita: The Tomita Parser Vs. Earley's Algorithm

Tomita (1985) compared his parser empirically with two versions of the Earley algorithm (E-I and E-II). In our terminology this would correspond to TD and TD+Sel. While the Tomita parser was producing a parse forest, E-I and E-II were run as recognizers and produced no parse.

In the comparison, four pure context-free phrase-structure grammars were used, consisting of a varying number of rules: G1, 8; G2, 40; G3, 220; and G4, 400 rules. These grammars were tested with two sets of sentences, S1: 40 sentences from texts and S2: 13 artificial sentences that have an increasing number of prepositional phrases (1 to 13). These artificial sentences are useful for testing growing sentence ambiguity since the number of parses grows exponentially (Martin et al. 1981).

---

10. "The early constituent test calls for the parser to evaluate that protion of the rule body-procedure which tests the first constituent, as soon as it is discovered, to determine if it is acceptable." (Slocum 1981b)

Tomita's experiment shows that his algorithm works 5 to 10 times faster than Earley's standard algorithm (TD), and 2 to 3 times faster than Earley's improved algorithm (TD+Sel). He states that this result is due to the pre-compilation of the grammar into an LR table. Tomita summarizes that his algorithm "is significantly faster than Earley's algorithm, in the context of practical natural language processing... Its parsing time and space remain tractable when sentence length, sentence ambiguity or grammar size grows in practical applications."

2.3.3. Wirén: Top-down and Bottom-up Chart Parsers, TD Vs. LC

Wirén compared in his experiment two basic chart parsers with several improvements, TD versus LC, both with selectivity, LC with top-down filtering.[11] He tested his parsers with grammars G1 to G3 from Tomita, with a reduced number of the two sentence sets S1 and S2.

The results of his experiments show that the "directed methods" – based on top-down filtering and selectivity – reduce significantly the number of edges and perform better than undirected parsers. Tested independently, the selectivity filter turned out to be much more time efficient than top-down filtering that degraded time performance as the grammar grew larger.[12] "The maximally directed strategy – ... with selectivity and top-down filtering – remained the most efficient one throughout all the experiments, both with respect to edges produced and time consumed." It performed better than TD with selectivity.

Putting the results of the three experiments together, we would expect that improved LC performs best amongst chart parsers. Since the Tomita parser has only been compared with TD, we can expect a different result by comparing it with improved bottom-up chart parsers that compile their rules into decision trees (cf. Section 2.2.1.4). Tomita and Wirén measure pure parsing time determined by CPU time minus time for garbage collection. Their grammars are pure CF grammars using little rule-body procedure time and it is therefore difficult to predict what the interaction will be between filtering overhead and rule-body procedure and how this will influence overall performance.

2.4. The Comparison

2.4.1. The Parsers

Our main goal was the selection of a suitable parsing strategy for our on-line MT-system. Since our application is time critical, one of the important

---

11. LC la Kilbury has already been used by Slocum. What it comes down to is that new active edges subsume the complete edges that have provoked their proposal. Since we use that variant of LC (cf. 2.2.1.1.2) coming from Slocum (1981a), we don't distinguish between a standard LC and the Kilbury variant.

12. Wirén explains this puzzle with implementational reasons.

questions was what combination of parser and rule-body procedure is best for our purpose. One of the objectives was to verify if the Tomita parser is as efficient as predicted if it is compared to improved bottom-up chart parsers. Since no comparison existed between all the basic rule invocation strategies for chart parsers, we decided to compare the Tomita parser with four chart parsers. To guarantee the comparability of the chart parsers, we chose Slocum's implementation (1981a) as basic design for all chart parsers. We added two supplementary rule invocation strategies to his bottom-up left-corner (LC) and Cocke-Kasami-Younger strategy (CKY), namely a top-down Earley-like strategy (TD) and a bi-directional strategy (BI). The basic chart parsers were augmented by two enhancements, i.e. top-down filtering and compilation of the rules into decision trees. We took the Tomita parser as described by Tomita (1985) and added a second version without the parse forest representation. Since its LR(0) parsing table has no lookahead, we added no lookahead to the chart parsers.

All the programs are implemented in Allegro Common Lisp and tested on a Macintosh II (MC68020 with 5 MB RAM). As main parameters we compared number of edges, number of rule-body procedure executions and over-all time.

2.4.2. The Grammars and Sentences

The first test uses small grammars (22 and 80 rules) together with the same 50 artificial sentences. The monadic grammars are tested with all 9 parsing strategies (TOM ±parse forest; TD, LC, CKY, BI, the bottom-up parsers ±Tdf), for features and unification grammars we use TOM without parse forest and all the chart parsers. The 50 test sentences are constructed artificially to control parameters like sentences ambiguity, sentences length and three linguistic phenomena, i.e. PP-attachment, relative clauses and coordination. They can be classified into two groups, one where ambiguity grows exponentially with increasing sentence length (PP-attachment and coordination), and a second group, where the sentence length does not influence ambiguity (they have 1 to 3 readings). The sentence length varies from 3 to 24 words. Each grammar type has two small grammars with approximately 25 resp. 80 rules.

The second test compares a reduced number of parsers (TOM, TD, LC, CKY, the bottom-up parsers ±Tdf) with a bigger monadic grammar based on the German avalanche corpus that has 750 rules and 300 lexical items. The 50 test sentences were taken from the avalanche corpus, their length varies from 6 to 42 words (average 19 words per sentence).

2.5. Test Results and Discussion

Before we comment, we will give a brief outline of how we present the test-results. Tables 2.1 through 2.3 summarize the statistics for each grammar and set of sentences. We give the total number of edges and the total time for each parser

Table 2.1. *Statistics for monadic grammers*

Monadic grammer: 22 rules

	edges	rank	diff	time all (ms)	rank	diff	ms/ word	time 2	rank	diff
lc+	6532	5	3.08	24049	2	1.67	38	8000	3	1.07
lc-	13332	8	6.28	41418	7	2.88	66	12301	6	1.64
cky+	3449	2	1.62	33219	4	2.31	53	12901	7	1.72
cky-	6886	6	3.24	34634	5	2.41	55	9599	4	1.28
bi+	6497	4	3.06	44483	8	3.10	71	15850	9	2.11
bi-	9655	7	4.55	36265	6	2.52	58	10033	5	1.34
td	19766	9	9.31	68217	9	4.75	109	12985	8	1.73
tom	2124	1	1.00	14364	1	1.00	23	7498	1	1.00
to-2	3881	3	1.83	25756	3	1.79	41	7940	2	1.06

Monadic grammer: 75 rules

	edges	rank	diff	time all (ms)	rank	diff	ms/ word	time 2	rank	diff
lc+	6224	5	3.38	24418	3	1.90	39	8417	6	1.36
lc-	9020	8	4.90	27834	6	2.16	44	7318	5	1.18
cky+	2803	2	1.52	38980	7	3.03	62	16481	7	2.66
cky-	4884	6	2.65	25650	4	1.99	41	6150	1	0.99
bi+	7476	4	4.06	56649	8	4.40	90	20084	8	3.24
bi-	8277	7	4.50	25815	5	2.00	41	6730	4	1.09
td	33028	9	17.95	84130	9	6.53	134	20665	9	3.33
tom	1840	1	1.00	12883	1	1.00	21	6200	2	1.00
to-2	3117	3	1.69	21899	2	1.70	35	6382	3	1.03

Monadic grammer: 750 rules

	edges	rank	diff	time all (ms)	rank	diff	ms/ word
lc+	3693	3	1.94	20132	2	1.28	21
lc-	18411	6	9.67	51132	6	3.26	54
cky+	1932	2	1.01	36715	4	2.34	39
cky-	6662	4	3.50	40785	5	2.60	43
td	16951	5	8.90	33717	3	2.15	35
tom	1904	1	1.00	15684	1	1.00	16

Abbreviations:

    +   with top-down filter

    -     without top-down filter

    tom Tomita + parse forest

    to-2 Tomita - parse forest

Table 2.2. *Statistics for feature grammers*

Feature grammer: 30 rules

	edges	rank	diff	time all (ms)	rank	diff	ms/ word	time 2	rank	diff
lc+	6067	4	2.10	38669	1	0.93	62	11434	2	1.06
lc-	12666	7	4.39	76415	6	1.85	122	18483	8	1.71
cky+	2661	1	0.92	47015	3	1.14	75	15233	4	1.41
cky-	5304	3	1.84	69844	5	1.69	111	16213	5	1.50
bi+	6165	5	2.14	64901	4	1.57	103	17517	7	1.62
bi-	10266	6	3.56	81869	7	1.98	130	14050	3	1.30
td	21669	8	7.52	114548	8	2.77	182	16982	6	1.57
to-2	2883	2	1.00	41368	2	1.00	66	10818	1	1.00

Feature grammer: 80 rules

	edges	rank	diff	time all (ms)	rank	diff	ms/ word	time 2	rank	diff
lc+	6232	4	2.02	41265	1	0.96	66	12383	3	1.04
lc-	8963	7	2.91	60867	6	1.42	97	14649	5	1.23
cky+	2831	1	0.92	57884	4	1.35	92	20668	6	1.73
cky-	4871	3	1.58	59248	5	1.38	94	13983	4	1.17
bi+	7459	5	2.42	80217	7	1.87	128	26467	8	2.22
bi-	8198	6	2.66	49901	3	1.16	79	11967	2	1.00
td	32792	8	10.64	135650	8	3.16	216	24985	7	2.10
to-2	3083	2	1.00	42985	2	1.00	68	11917	1	1.00

over all sentences. The figures for time indicate overall time[13] that includes rule-body procedure etc. The reader should be careful in the interpretation of the timings; these figures are dependent on machine, lisp system and the way in which the algorithms are programmed. Nevertheless, we think that they give an indication of relations. Figure 2.1 through 2.5 shows a limited number of diagrams to illustrate the figures graphically.

In Tables 2.1 through 2.3, each table shows three fields, one for the number of edges and two for timings: 1) The "time all"-field gives the total time for all artificial sentences, resp. the avalanche sentences. 2) The "time 2"-field indicates the time for the subset of the 26 sentences with low ambiguity. The second group of test sentences includes relative clauses and coordinations. The number of words per sentence goes from 5 to 23 words (13 average) and they have 1 to 5 readings. Time is measured in milliseconds. The column "diff" indicates the difference of the parsers from Tomita which is set to 1. In the field "time all," we have added the average time per word (ms/word) in order to have a figure that can easily be compared across the different tests. We have

---

13. Since we have forced a garbage collection before each sentence, the garbage collector does not interfere with the timings.

Table 2.3. *Statistics for unification grammers*

Unification grammer: 30 rules									
	edges	rank	diff	time all (ms)	rank	diff	ms/ word	time 2	rank	diff
lc+	5449	3	1.79	144349	1	0.91	251	23433	1	0.93
lc-	11446	6	3.75	525250	7	3.32	913	74750	8	2.97
cky+	2813	1	0.92	153500	2	0.97	267	27233	3	1.08
cky-	7068	4	2.32	533515	8	3.38	928	73167	7	2.91
bi+	8675	5	2.85	210300	5	1.33	366	29034	5	1.16
bi-	14247	7	4.67	307949	6	1.95	536	37866	6	1.51
td	18795	8	6.16	169684	4	1.07	295	27983	4	1.11
to-2	3049	2	1.00	158032	3	1.00	275	25132	2	1.00

Unification grammer: 80 rules									
	edges	rank	diff	time all (ms)	rank	diff	ms/ word	time 2	rank	diff
lc+	5519	3	2.00	108382	1	0.95	188	20531	2	1.03
lc-	12527	7	4.54	272181	8	2.39	473	42549	8	2.14
cky+	2483	1	0.90	122618	3	1.08	213	27603	3	1.39
cky-	5700	4	2.07	268468	7	2.36	467	41485	7	2.09
bi+	6770	5	2.45	135834	4	1.19	236	29918	4	1.51
bi-	12232	6	4.43	189650	6	1.67	330	30217	5	1.52
td	34093	8	12.36	146203	5	1.29	254	31551	6	1.59
to-2	2759	2	1.00	113750	2	1.00	198	19866	1	1.00

listed the number of edges because this figure is often given as measurement for parser performance. But one can observe that the rankings based on the number of edges and the one based on timing do not correspond. This is due to the particular way in which the chart parsers are implemented. As we have mentioned in Section 2.2.1.1, TD and LC keep only active edges in the chart, whereas CKY has only complete edges and BI both. For TOM, we counted the number of shift operations.

The diagrams in Figures 2.1 through 2.5 show three parsers: TOM, TD and LC ±Tdf. All the diagrams display the time/word relation for a particular grammar and a sentence set. Figures 2.1 and 2.2 show PP-attachment (high ambiguity: a 20 word sentence has 132 parses), Figure 2.3 the time/word relation for the 750 rule grammar and all the avalanche sentences. Figure 2.4 represents the times for LC ±Tdf with the three different grammar types for a set of coordinations in high ambiguity. Figure 2.5 shows all parsers with a set of relative clauses that have low ambiguity.

2.5.1. The Chart Parsers

Our tests confirm Slocum's and Wirén's data: the left-corner parser (LC) with

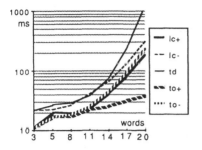

Figure 2.1. Monad-22 PP-attachment.

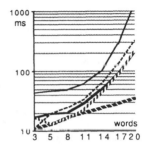

Figure 2.2. Monad-75 PP-attachment.

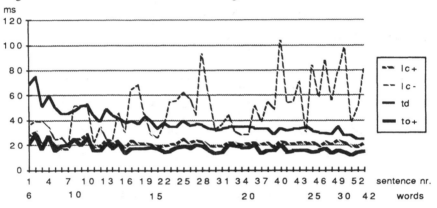

Figure 2.3. Monadic-750 (all sentences).

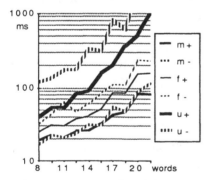

Figure 2.4. LC ±tdf (30 rules)
3 grammer types, coordination,
high ambiguity.

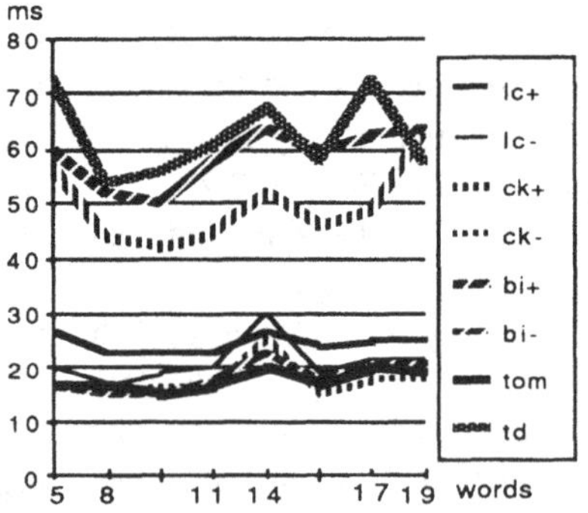

Figure 2.5. Monadic-75, relative clauses,
low ambiguity.

top-down filtering is overall the most efficient chart parser. It ranks highest among the chart parsers with all grammar types and grammar sizes. The only exceptions are monadic and feature grammars of the size of 80 rules with low ambiguity sentences (see below 2.5.3.). Earley-like top-down (TD) with the two small grammars is highly overproductive in active edges and therefore a bad choice if it is used without selectivity. Figure 2.1 and 2.2 show how TD is influenced negatively by the grammar size, the grammar in Figure 2.2 has three times more rules. Strangely enough, in the large grammar (Table 2.1, part 3, and Figure 2.3), TD is converging towards LC as the sentences grow longer. In Figure 2.3, one can see well its initial overhead of active edges.

The bi-directional chart parser (BI) was included in the tests for verifying the hypothesis if triggering annotations on the rules reduce the search space and improve the overall performance. None of our tests could confirm such a hypothesis. It seems that top-down filtering or selectivity influence performance to a greater extent than linguistic triggering annotations. BI did not perform better with any particular set of test sentences or grammars.

2.5.2. The Tomita Parser and Chart Parsers

Figures 2.1 and 2.2 show how the Tomita parser (to+) performs best in situations of high ambiguity. Taking the overall timings in Table 2.1, parts 1 and 2, TD is 4.75 to 6.53 times slower than TOM (and our comparison stops at sentences with 20 words with 132 readings). The situation is less dramatic if we take LC+Tdf. Here the difference is 1.67 to 1.9. But, if we take our grammar of 750 rules with its low ambiguity sentences, the gap is much smaller: 1.38 for LC+Tdf and 2.15 for TD. A closer look at Figures 2.1 and 2.2 shows that TOM without parse forest (to-) is roughly equivalent to LC+Tdf (lc+). We therefore think that the major speed gain of TOM comes from its parse forest, which is an efficient way of packing the parse trees. But, this representation could be used with any parser and is not specific of TOM. In Figure 2.3, TOM and LC+Tdf show a constant time difference. Precompiling the grammar rules into a LR parsing table or precompiling them into decision trees does not make a crucial difference, even with very long sentences of up to 42 words and a large grammar of 750 rules.

2.5.3. Filters, Grammar Size and Rule-Body Procedures

This chapter tries to address the complex interaction between parsing strategy, grammar size, sentence ambiguity and overheads for top-down filtering and rule-body procedure. There is no standard grammar size. According to the grammar type, the size varies. We estimate that unification grammars, which are highly lexical, might have 50 to 100 rules, grammars with simple features around 500,[14] and monadic grammars several thousand rules.

In general, a TD parser is disadvantaged if the grammar has a high branching factor because of its overproduction of active edges (cf. Section 2.2.1.3.).

---

14. The Metal German analysis grammar, which is based on simple features, has 500-600 rules.

Bottom-up parsers suffer from rules with common right factoring in the right-hand side of the rules (cf. Section 2.2.1.2.). A grammar might produce different results about TD overproduction or top-down filters according to its branching factor or right factoring. The effect of a top-down filter is not always a good one. We have contradicting results about top-down filtering. In the test with the monadic grammar of 750 rules, the two chart parsers with top-down filter (lc+ and cky+) perform better than their counterparts without filter. Figure 2.3 also shows a converging TD and a diverging LC-Tdf (lc-) as the sentence length increases. This is due to the high right factoring of that grammar. The opposite result is shown by monadic and feature grammars with 75 rules together with the sample of low ambiguity sentences. In these cases, the overhead from the top-down filter deteriorates the efficiency of the chart parsers with top-down filter. Unfiltered parsers with sentences up to 19 words are faster than the filtered ones. This result is influenced by the nature of the grammar as well as its size since the top-down filter with the small grammars (22 or 30 rules) shows a positive effect.

Another tradeoff is between top-down filter and rule-body procedure. In our tests we compare three different types of rule-body procedures: no annotations in monadic grammars or simple features and unification. Monadic grammars and simple feature grammars have a small rule-body procedure whereas the overhead for unification is considerable (2/3 for unification and 1/3 for pure parsing). Figure 2.4 shows optically that the top-down filter has a positive effect as the rule-body procedure grows. With a time consuming rule-body procedure, a top-down filter becomes vital for the overall efficiency. This statement should not be interpreted as a generalization about simple feature grammars versus unification. Our point is independent of a particular grammar type but has to do with the relation between pure parse time and rule-body procedure time.

2.5.4. Sentence Length

As we reported in Section 2.3.1, Slocum claims that the benefits of top-down filtering are dependent on the sentence length and that the break-even point for top-down filtering (averaged over LC and CKY) occurs at about 7 words. As we have shown above, the question is more complex and influenced furthermore by the number of parses as well as by the nature and by the size of the grammar (right factoring and branching factor). Some of our tests show clearly that the length of the sentence is not necessarily the main parameter. We believe that no generalization is possible unless all the mentioned factors are taken into account.

2.5.5. Final Choice

The choice of the parsing strategy for our MT-system was guided by the following ideas: Possible candidates for an on-line parser that parses strictly from left to right are TOM, LC+Tdf and TD. Given the performance, TD was ruled out. The question of the grammar type was more difficult to solve. The grammar has to predict all the sentences but only the correct ones, no overproduction is allowed. We therefore have to subclassify heavily by using a system of about 100 grammatical and semantic features. The worst cases for an empirical efficiency test are sentences with high ambiguity. Figure 2.4 shows the performance of the three grammar types where the 20 word sentence has the highest ambiguity. The average time per word varies heavily according to the grammar type: monadic – 70 ms, features – 160 ms and unification – 1267 ms. Unification is slower by a factor of about 20. This factor would be increased by the search for possible next words because it is not a simple matching of categories but a complicated search that has to take into account all the instantiated variables from constituents that have already been found. Given this poor expectation for unification grammar in on-line parsing, we were left with two grammar types, and we opted for simple monadic grammars, rather as a matter of computational simplicity. Together with monadic grammars, we chose the Tomita parser, because it was slightly more performant with the large grammar for the avalanche corpus, and last but not least, because of its elegance. We like the idea of precompiling the grammar into a LR table.

2.6. Concluding Remarks

We have come to the conclusion that it is very difficult to test empirically the performance of algorithms or better of programs and to find good generalizations.[15] Nevertheless, we believe that we have shown that the parse forest representation is to a large extent responsible for the good performance of the Tomita parser, and second, that the difference in efficiency between the Tomita parser without the parse forest representation and an enhanced left-corner parser with top-down filtering and compiled rules is small. Two points of empirical research have not been addressed in our tests, which could also help the practitioners of computational linguistics when they have to select their parsing strategies: 1) We have excluded the use of a lookahead. We think that this point needs further investigation (i.e. TOM with an LALR table versus LC+Tdf with La). 2) Since the parse forest representation is highly efficient, its benefits in combination with unification grammars need more clarification.

Acknowledgements

I would like to thank Anne De Roeck and Tony Lawson for all the theoretical and practical discussions as well as for the contribution of the unification grammar from Anne and the unifyer from Tony. Thanks also to Mike Rosner, Rod

---

15. On a different machine with a different lisp system the same programs might behave differently.

Johnson, Dominique Petitpierre and Thomas Russi for their comments and useful hints.

References

Aho, A. & and Ullman, J., 1979, *Principles of compiler design*, Addison Wesly.

Earley, J., 1970, "An efficient context-free parsing algorithm," *Communications of the ACM*, 13(2), 94-102.

Kay, M., 1982, *Algorithmic schemata and data structures in syntactic processing*, CSL-80-12, Xerox Parc, Palo Alto.

Martin, W., Church, K., & R. Patil, 1981, *Preliminary analysis of a breadth-first parsing algorithm: Theoretical and experimental results*, MIT LCS Technical report.

Pratt, V., 1975, "LINGOL - A progress report," *Proc. 4th IJCAI*, Tbilisi, 422-428.

Slocum, J., 1981a, *A practical comparison of parsing strategies for machine translation and other natural language processing purposes*, PhD University of Texas, Austin.

Slocum, J., 1981b, "A practical comparison of parsing strategies," Proc. 19th ACL, Standford.

Steel, S. & De Roeck, A., 1987, *Bi-directional parsing*, in Hallam & Mellish (eds.), *Advances in AI, Proc. of the 1987 AISB Conference*, J. Wiley, London.

Tennant, H. R., et al., 1983, "Menu-based natural language understanding," Proc. 21st ACL, 151-158.

Thompson, H., 1981, "Chart parsing and rule schemata in GPSG," Proc. 19th ACL, Stanford.

Tomita, M., 1985, *An efficient context-free parsing algorithm for natural languages and its applications*, PhD CMU, Pittsburg. Also as: Efficient parsing for natural language. A fast algorithm for practical purposes. Kluwer, Boston, 1986.

Tomita, M., 1987, "An efficient augmented-context-free parsing algorithm," *Computational Linguistics*, 13(1/2).

Tomita, M., 1988, "Graph-structured stack and natural language parsing," *Proc. 26th ACL*, Buffalo.

Winograd, J., 1983, "Language as a cognitive process," *Syntax*, Addison-Wesley.

Wirén, M., 1987, "A comparison of rule-invocation strategies in context-free chart parsing," *Proc. 3rd European chapter ACL*, 226- 233.

3 The Computational Complexity of GLR Parsing

Mark Johnson

3.1. Introduction

The Tomita parsing algorithm adapts Knuth's (1967) well-known parsing algorithm for LR(k) grammars to non-LR grammars, including ambiguous grammars. Knuth's algorithm is provably efficient: it requires at most $O(n|G|)$ units of time, where $|G|$ is the size of (i.e. the number of symbols in) G and n is the length of the string to be parsed. This is often significantly better than the $O(n^3|G|^2)$ worst case time required by standard parsing algorithms such as the Earley algorithm. Since the Tomita algorithm is closely related to Knuth's algorithm, one might expect that it too is provably more efficient than the Earley algorithm, especially as actual computational implementations of Tomita's algorithm outperform implementations of the Earley algorithm (Tomita 1986, 1987).

This chapter shows that this is not the case. Two main results are presented in this chapter. First, for any m there is a grammar L_m such that Tomita's algorithm performs $\Omega(n^m)$ operations to parse a string of length n. Second, there is an infinite sequence of distinct grammars G_m such that Tomita's algorithm performs $\Omega(nc^{\sqrt{|G_m|}})$ operations to parse a string of length n. Thus it is not the case that the Tomita algorithm is always more efficient than Earley's algorithm; rather there are grammars for which it is exponentially slower. This result is forshadowed in Tomita (1986, p. 72), where the author remarks that Tomita's algorithm can require time proportional to more than the cube of the input length. The result showing that the Tomita parser can require time proportional to a non-polynomially-bounded function of the grammar size is new, as far as I can tell.[1]

3.2. The Tomita Parsing Algorithm

This section briefly describes the relevant aspects of the Tomita parsing algorithm: for further details see Tomita (1986). Familiarity with Knuth's LR

---

1. Robert Berwick informs me that similiar results are presented in David A. Chanen's June 1986 MIT EECS B.S. thesis entitled "The use of concurrency with modified LR(k) methods." I have not been able to obtain a copy of this thesis.

parsing algorithm is presumed: see the original article by Knuth (1967), Aho and Ullman (1972), or Aho, Sethi and Ullman (1986) for details.

The Tomita algorithm and Knuth's LR parsing algorithm on which it is based are both shift-reduce parsing algorithms, and both use the same LR automaton to determine the parsing actions to be performed. The LR automaton is not always deterministic: for example, if the grammar is ambiguous then at some point in the analysis of an ambiguous string two different parsing actions must be possible that lead to the two distinct analyses of that string. Knuth's algorithm is only defined for grammars for which the parsing automaton is deterministic: these are called the $LR(k)$ grammars, where k is the length of the lookahead strings. Tomita's algorithm extends Knuth's to deal with non-deterministic LR automata.

Tomita's algorithm in effect simulates non-determinism by computing *all* of the LR stacks that result from each of the actions of a non-deterministic LR automaton state. Tomita's algorithm mitigates the cost of this non-determinism by representing the set of all the LR stacks possible at a given point of the parse as a multiply-rooted directed acyclic graph called a *graph-structured stack*, which is very similiar to a parsing chart (Tomita 1988). Each node of this graph represents an LR state of one or more of the LR stacks, with the root nodes representing the top states of LR parse stacks. The graph contains exactly one leaf node (i.e. a node with no successors). This leaf node represents the start state of the LR automata (since this is the bottom element of all LR parse stacks), and each maximal path through the graph (i.e. from a root to the leaf) represents an LR parse stack.

As each item in the input string is read all of the parsing actions called for by the top state of each LR stack are performed, resulting in a new set of LR stacks. Because of the way in which the set of LR stacks are represented, Tomita's algorithm avoids the need to copy the each LR stack in its entirety at non-deterministic LR automaton states; rather the top elements of the two (or more) new stacks are represented by nodes whose successors are the nodes that represent the LR stack elements they have in common. Similiarly, if the same LR state appears as the top element of two or more new stacks then these elements are represented by a single node whose immediate successors are the set of nodes that represent the other elements of these LR stacks. This "merging" of identical top elements of distinct LR stacks allows Tomita's algorithm to avoid duplicating the same computation in different contexts.

Finally, Tomita employs a *packed forest* representation of the parse trees in order to avoid enumerating these trees, the number of which can grow exponentially as a function of input length. In this representation there is at most one node of a given category at any string location (i.e. a pair of beginning and ending string positions), so the number of nodes in such a packed forest is at most proportional to the square of the input length. Each node is associated with a set of sequences of descendant nodes where each sequence represents one

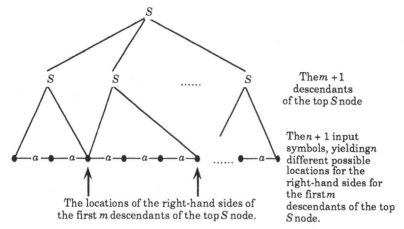

The $m + 1$ descendants of the top S node

The $n + 1$ input symbols, yielding n different possible locations for the right-hand sides for the first m descendants of the top S node.

The locations of the right-hand sides of the first m descendants of the top S node.

Figure 3.1. Parse Trees generated by grammar L_m.

possible expansion of the node; thus the trees represented can easily be "read off" the packed forest representation.

3.3. Complexity as a Function of Input Length

The rest of this chapter shows the complexity results claimed above. This section describes a sequence of grammars L_m such that on sufficiently long inputs the Tomita algorithm performs more than $\Omega(n^m)$ operations to parse an input of length n. This result follows from properties of the packed forest representation alone, so it applies to *any* algorithm that constructs packed forest representations of parse trees.

Consider the sequence of grammars L_m for $m > 0$ defined in (3.1), where S^{m+2} abbreviates a sequence of S's of length $m + 2$.

$$S \rightarrow a$$
$$S \rightarrow SS \tag{3.1}$$
$$S \rightarrow S^{m+2}$$

All of these grammars generate the same language, namely the set of strings a^+. Consider the input string a^{n+1} for $n > m$. By virtue of the first two rules in (3.1) any non-empty substring of the input can be analyzed as an S. Thus the number of different sequences of descendant nodes of the matrix or top-most S node licensed by the third rule in (3.1) is $\binom{n}{m+1}$, the number of ways of choosing different right string positions of the top-most S node's first $m + 1$ descendants. Since $\binom{n}{m+1}$ is a polynomial in n of order $m+1$, it is bounded below by cn^m for some $c > 0$ and sufficiently large n, i.e. $\binom{n}{m+1} = \Omega(n^m)$. Figure 3.1 sketches the structure of the relevant parse trees. Since any algorithm which uses the packed forest representation, such as Tomita's algorithm, requires the construction of these sequences of descendant nodes, any such algorithm must perform $\Omega(n^m)$ operations.

Finally, it should be noted that this result assumes that the sequences of descendant nodes are completely enumerated. Billot and Lang (1989) show that it is possible to "pack" these sequences in such a fashion that avoids their enumeration, allowing packed forest representations to be constructed in polynomial time.

3.4. Complexity as a Function of Grammar Size

This section shows that there are some grammars such that the total number of operations performed by the Tomita algorithm is an exponential function of the size of the grammar.

The amount of work involved in processing a single input item is proportional to the number of distinct top states of the set of LR stacks corresponding to the different non-deterministic analyses of the portion of the input string shown so far. By exhibiting a sequence of grammars in which the number of such states is an exponential function of the size of the grammar we show that the total number of operations performed by the Tomita algorithm can be at least exponentially related to the size of the grammar.

Consider the sequence of grammars G_m for $m > 0$ defined in (3.2).[2]

$$
\begin{aligned}
S &\rightarrow A_i & 0 \leq i \leq m \\
A_i &\rightarrow B_j A_i & 0 \leq i, j \leq m, i \neq j \\
A_i &\rightarrow B_j & 0 \leq i, j \leq m, i \neq j \\
B_j &\rightarrow a & 0 \leq j \leq m
\end{aligned}
\tag{3.2}
$$

All of the grammars G_m generate the same language, namely the set of strings a^+. Since these grammars are ambiguous they are not LR(k) for any k.

Consider the behaviour of a non-deterministic LR parser for the grammar G_m on an input string a^n where $n > m$. The items of the start state are shown in (3.3).

$$
\begin{bmatrix}
S \rightarrow \cdot A_i \\
A_i \rightarrow \cdot B_j A_i \\
A_i \rightarrow \cdot B_j \\
B_j \rightarrow \cdot a
\end{bmatrix}
\qquad 0 \leq i, j \leq m; i \neq j
\tag{3.3}
$$

The parser shifts over the first input symbol a to the state shown in (3.4).

$$
\begin{bmatrix} B_j \rightarrow a \cdot \end{bmatrix} \qquad 0 \leq j \leq m
\tag{3.4}
$$

---

2. These grammars are based on the grammars in exercise 4.41 of Aho, Seithi and Ullman (1986), which were brought to my attention by Fernando Pereira.

This is a non-deterministic state, since all of the m reductions $B_j \rightarrow a$ are possible parsing actions from this state. Suppose that the reduction to B_{k_1} is chosen. The state that results from the reduction to B_{k_1} is shown in (3.5). There are m such states.

$$
\begin{bmatrix}
A_i \rightarrow B_{k_1} \cdot A_i \\
A_i \rightarrow B_{k_1} \cdot \\
A_i \rightarrow \cdot B_j A_i \\
A_i \rightarrow \cdot B_j \\
B_j \rightarrow \cdot a
\end{bmatrix}
\qquad 0 \leq i, j, k_1 \leq m; i \neq j, k_1 \qquad (3.5)
$$

After shifting over the next input symbol the parser again reaches the same ambiguous state as before, namely the state shown in (3.4). Suppose the reduction to B_{k_2} is chosen. If $B_{k_1} = B_{k_2}$ then the resulting state is the one shown in (3.5). On the other hand, if $B_{k_1} \neq B_{k_2}$ then the resulting state is as shown in (3.6). There are $m(m-1)/2$ distinct states of the form shown in (3.6), so after reducing B_{k_2} there will be $m(m+1)/2$ distinct LR states in all.

$$
\begin{bmatrix}
A_i \rightarrow B_{k_2} \cdot A_i \\
A_i \rightarrow B_{k_2} \cdot \\
A_i \rightarrow \cdot B_j A_i \\
A_i \rightarrow \cdot B_j \\
B_j \rightarrow \cdot a
\end{bmatrix}
\qquad 0 \leq i, j, k_1, k_2 \leq m; i \neq j, k_1, k_2 \qquad (3.6)
$$

It is not hard to see that after $n \geq m$ input symbols have been read and reduced to $B_{k_1} \ldots B_{k_n}$ respectively the resulting state will be as shown in (3.7).

$$
\begin{bmatrix}
A_i \rightarrow B_{k_n} \cdot A_i \\
A_i \rightarrow B_{k_n} \cdot \\
A_i \rightarrow \cdot B_j A_i \\
A_i \rightarrow \cdot B_j \\
B_j \rightarrow \cdot a
\end{bmatrix}
\qquad 0 \leq i, j \leq m; i \neq j, k_1 \ldots k_n \qquad (3.7)
$$

Since there are $2^m - 1$ distinct such states, the Tomita parser must perform at least $2^m - 1$ computations per input item after the first m items have been read. Since $|G_m| = 5m^2 - m = O(m^2)$, the ratio of the average number of computations per input item for a sufficiently long string to grammar size is $\Omega(c^{\sqrt{|G_m|}})$ for some $c > 1$. Thus the total number of operations performed by the parser to parse a string of length n is $\Omega(nc^{\sqrt{|G_m|}})$, an non-polynomial function of grammar size.[3]

---

3. I would like to thank Andreas Eisele for pointing out an error in this section in earlier versions of this paper.

3.5. Concluding Remarks

The results just demonstrated show that Tomita's algorithm is not always faster that Earley's algorithm, but can be exponentially slower. As noted in the text, it is probably straight-forward to modify Tomita's algorithm so that it uses the techniques of Billot and Lang (1989) that pack subsequences of descendant nodes in the packed tree representation, and hence requires only polynomial time to recognize the grammars presented in Section 3.3 above.

It does not seem so straight-forward to modify Tomita's algorithm so that it does not require time proportional to the exponential of the grammar size for the grammars presented in Section 3.4. This is because this time requirement follows simply from the number of LR states "active" at any point in the parse, rather than a property of the data structures or representations employed by the algorithm. Any modification that does not require exponential time would probably have to replace the LR automaton that the Tomita algorithm uses.

It is important to note that the result of Section 3.4 describes the computational complexity of the Tomita algorithm with respect to grammar size. In many intended applications of the algorithm the grammar is fixed and hence the grammar size is a constant, so the exponential increases in computational complexity would not occur. But if Barton, Berwick and Ristad (1987) are correct that the *universal parsing problem* is the appropriate formulation of the computational complexity for natural language parsing, then such grammar-size complexity results are important considerations in computational linguistics.

Of course the exponential increase in computational complexity with respect to grammar size occurs only with certain sequences of grammars; a sequence of LR(k) grammars would not exhibit it, of course. Two properties are required for the exponential increase in computational complexity exhibited by the grammars in Section 3.4, namely:

- The LR automaton must have a large number of states. Since an LR state characterizes the "left context" of the current parse configuration, this means that there must be a large number of distinct left contexts (in the grammars of Section 3.4, these are the subsets of the categories B_i).
- A large number of these LR states must be valid at many points of the input string. This means that some input prefixes must be highly (locally) ambiguous.

As far as I know, it is not known whether all grammars that cause an exponential increase in computational complexity with respect to grammar size in Tomita's algorithm have these properties.

It is interesting to speculate as to why computational implementations of Tomita's algorithm are reported to outperform Earley's algorithm for various natural language grammar fragments (Tomita 1986, 1987).

It is possible that the average time complexity (over the whole class of context-free grammars) is superior to the Earley algorithm, even though its worst-case behaviour is inferior, and the results reported in the literature merely reflect this fact.

It is also possible that implementation details of the algorithms, e.g. the type of indexing employed, etc., could be responsible for the performance differences, and the reported results might be reflecting these details, rather than properties of the algorithms per se. It could be argued that Earley's algorithm, formulated to theoretically establish an $O(n^3)$ complexity bound for context-free parsing, is not an appropriate algorithm for implementation comparision with Tomita's algorithm—a tabular algorithm designed to reduce average total parse time, such as the one described by Graham et. al. 1980, might be a more appropriate choice.

However, the most intriguing hypothesis is that the class of grammars efficiently parsable by Tomita's algorithm includes the class of natural language grammars. There is some reason to believe that this may be the case, since shift-reduce parsers have been claimed to accurately model various aspects of human language processing (see Berwick and Weinberg 1984, Pereira 1985 and Shieber 1983 for arguments in favour of this position; for contrary arguments see Abney and Johnson forthcoming).

Finally, it is important to stress that Earley's and Tomita's algorithms do not exhaust the space of possible parsing algorithms. Lang 1988 describes a framework which can abstractly characterize both of these algorithms, and makes it clear that there are many other parsing algorithms still waiting to be explored.

Acknowledgements

Stephen Abney, Robert Berwick, Andreas Eisele, Aravind Joshi, Martin Kay, Fernando Pereira, Stuart Shieber and Masaru Tomita all made helpful suggestions regarding this chapter. All errors remain my own, however.

References

Abney and Johnson (forthcoming) *Eager Parsing*, paper to be presented at the 1990 CUNY Conference on Sentence Processing, CUNY, New York.

Aho and Ullman (1972) *The Theory of Parsing, Translation and Compiling*, vol. 1, Prentice Hall, New Jersey.

Aho, Sethi and Ullman (1986) *Compilers: Principles, Techniques and Tools*, Addison-Wesley, Reading, Mass.

Barton, Berwick and Ristad (1987) *Computational Complexity and Natural Language*, The MIT Press, Cambridge, Mass.

Berwick and Weinberg (1984) *The Grammatical Basis of Linguistic Performance*, The MIT Press, Cambridge, Mass.

Billot and Lang (1989) "The Structure of Shared Forests in Ambiguous Parsing", *Proceedings of the 27th Annual Meeting of the Association for Computational Linguistics*, Vancouver, Canada.

Graham, Harrison and Ruzzo (1980) "An Improved Context-Free Recognizer", *ACM Transactions on Programming Languages and Systems*, vol. 2, no. 3, pages 415–462.

Pereira (1985), "A New Characterization of Attachment Preferences", in Dowty, Karttunen and
    Zwicky, eds., *Natural Language Parsing*, Cambridge University Press, Cambridge, England.
Lang, (1988) *Complete Evaluation of Horn Clauses: An Automata Theoretic Approach*, INRIA
    Report 913, France.
Shieber (1983), "Sentence Disambiguation by a Shift-Reduce Parsing Technique", ACL Proceedings,
    The 21st Annual Meeting of the ACL.
Tomita (1986) *Efficient Parsing for Natural Language*, Kluwer, Boston, Mass.
Tomita (1987) "An Efficient Augmented-Context-Free Parsing Algorithm", *Computational Linguis-
    tics*, vol. 13, 31-46.
Tomita (1988) "Graph-Structured Stack and Natural Language Parsing", in *The Proceedings of the
    26th Annual Meeting of the Association for Computational Linguistics*, SUNY Buffalo, New
    York.

4   GLR Parsing in Time O(n^3)

James R. Kipps

4.1. Introduction

Algorithms for general CF parsing, e.g., Earley's algorithm (Earley, 1968) and the Cocke-Younger-Kasami algorithm (Younger, 1967), are necessarily less efficient than algorithms for restricted CF parsing, e.g., the LL, operator precedence, and LR algorithms (Aho and Ullman, 1972), because they must simulate a multi-path, nondeterministic pass over their inputs using some form of search, typically, goal-driven. While many of the general algorithms can be shown to theoretically perform as well as the restricted algorithms on a large subclass of CF grammars, due to the inefficiency of goal expansion the general algorithms have not been widely used as practical parsers for programming languages.

A basic characteristic shared by many of the best known general algorithms is that they are top-down parsers. Tomita's algorithm (Tomita, 1985) can be distinguished from other general algorithms because it is defined as a variation of standard LR parsing, which makes it a table-driven, bottom-up parser. The benefit of this approach is that it eliminates the need to expand alternatives of a nonterminal at parse time (what Earley refers to as the predictor operation).

For Earley's algorithm, eliminating the predictor operation does not change the algorithm's time bound of O(n^3). However, the predictor operation does account for proportional to n^2 steps when parsing a string of length n.[1] Eliminating these steps could have a significant impact to practical parsing applications. Thus, it is of interest to analyze the complexity of Tomita's algorithm.

Upon examination, Tomita's algorithm is found to have a general time complexity of O($n^{\bar{p}+1}$), where n is the length of the input string and $\bar{p}$ is the length of the longest production in the grammar. Tomita's algorithm achieves O(n^3) time for grammars in Chomsky normal form (Chomsky, 1959) but has potential for being worse when productions are of unrestricted length. In this chapter, I present a modification of Tomita's algorithm that allows it to run in time proportional to n^3 for grammars with productions of arbitrary length.

4.2. Tomita's Algorithm

Tomita's algorithm is a variation on standard LR parsing. It takes a shift-reduce

---

1. A bounded number of steps for each of $\sim i$ states in each state set S_i, for i from 1 to n.

$$
\begin{aligned}
(1)\quad & S \;\rightarrow\; S\ S\ S \\
(2)\quad & S \;\rightarrow\; S\ x \\
(3)\quad & S \;\rightarrow\; x
\end{aligned}
$$

Figure 4.1. Example non-LR grammar.

State	x	⊣	S
0	sh2		go1
1	sh4	acc	go3
2	re3	re3	
3	sh4		go5
4	re2,re3	re2,re3	
5	sh4,re1	re1	go5

Figure 4.2. Extended LR parse table.

approach, using an extended LR parse table to guide its actions. In the extended parse table, shift/reduce and reduce/reduce conflicts are recorded as multiple action entries. As a result, the parse table cannot be used deterministically, i.e., without some form of search. The algorithm simulates a nondeterministic parse with pseudo-parallelism. It scans an input string $x_1 \cdots x_n$ from left to right, following all paths in a breath-first manner and merging like subpaths when possible to avoid redundant computations.

4.2.1. The Extended LR Parse Table

To illustrated the nature and use of the extended LR parse table, consider the simple non-LR(k) grammar shown in Figure 4.1. In this grammar, there is only one nonterminal symbol, S, and one terminal, x. The language described by this grammar is the set of all strings of x's. This grammar is of general interest because it forces Tomita's algorithm to exhibit worst-case behavior.

The extended LR parse table constructed from our grammar is shown in Figure 4.2. In building the parser table the grammar is augmented by a 0th production $R \rightarrow S \dashv$, where R is the root of the grammar and '⊣' is the end-of-sentence symbol, which only appears as the last symbol of the input string.

Entries sh$s$ in the action table indicate the action 'Shift to state s.' Entries re$p$ indicate the action 'Reduce constituents on the stack according to production p.' The entry acc indicates the action 'Accept,' and blanks indicate 'Error.' Entries go$s$ in the goto table indicate the action 'After a reduce action, shift to state s.' In Figure 4.2, there are three multi-action entries in states 4 and 5.

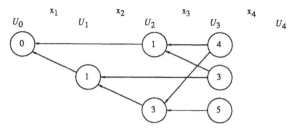

Figure 4.3. Example graph-structured stack.

4.2.2. The Graph-Structured Stack

Tomita's algorithm operates by maintaining a number of parsing processes in parallel. Each process has a stack, scans the input string from left-to-right, and, thus, behaves basically the same as the single parsing process in a standard LR parser. Each stack element is labeled with a parse state and points to its parent, i.e., the previous element on a process's stack. We refer to the top-of-stack as the current state of a process.

Each process does not actually maintain its own separate stack. Rather, these "multiple" stacks are represented using a single directed acyclic (but reentrant) graph called a *graph-structured stack*, an example of which is shown in Figure 4.3.

Each stack element corresponds to a vertex of the graph. (In Figure 4.3, circles represent the vertices of the graph; each circle is labeled with a parse state.) Each leaf of the graph acts as a distinct top-of-stack to a process. (There are three processes depicted in Figure 4.3: one in state 4, one in state 3, and one in state 5.) The root of the graph acts as a common bottom-of-stack. The edge between a vertex and its parent is directed toward the parent. Because of the reentrant nature of the graph, as explained below, a vertex may have more than one parent. (In Figure 4.3, the vertex in state 3 under U_3 has two parent vertices.)

The leaves of the graph grow in stages. Each stage U_i corresponds to the ith symbol x_i from the input string. After x_i is scanned, the leaves in stage U_i are in a one-to-one correspondence with the algorithm's *active* processes, where each process references a distinct leaf of the graph and treats that leaf as its current state. Upon scanning x_{i+1}, an active process can either (1) add an additional leaf to U_i, or (2) add a leaf to U_{i+1}. Only processes that have added leaves to U_{i+1} will be active when x_{i+2} is scanned. (In Figure 4.3, x_4 is being scanned. By executing two reduce actions, the process in state 4 has added two new leaves to U_3, i.e., the processes in state 3 and state 5; no leaves have yet been added to U_4.)

4.2.3. The Parsing Process

In general, a process behaves in the following manner. On x_i, each active process (corresponding to the leaves in U_{i-1}) executes the entries in the action table for x_i given its current state. When a process encounters multiple actions, it *splits* into several processes (one for each action), each sharing a common top-of-stack. (In Figure 4.3, the process in state 4 has two reduce actions, causing it to split.) When a process encounters an error entry, the process is discarded. All processes are synchronized, scanning the same symbol at the same time. After a process shifts on x_i into U_i, it waits until there are no other processes that can act on x_i before scanning x_{i+1}.

The Shift Action. A process (with top-of-stack vertex v) shifts on x_i from its current state s to some successor state s' by

1. creating a new leaf v' in U_i labeled s';
2. placing an edge from v' to its top-of-stack v (directed towards v);
3. making v' its new top-of-stack vertex (in this way changing its current state).

Any successive process shifting to the same state s' in U_i is *merged* with the existing process to form a single process whose top-of-stack vertex has multiple parents, i.e., by placing an additional edge from the top-of-stack vertex of the existing process in U_i to the top-of-stack vertex of the shifting process. The merge is done because, individually, these processes would behave in exactly the same manner until a reduce action removed the vertices labeled s' from their stacks. Thus, merging avoids redundant computation. Merging also ensures that each leaf in any U_i will be labeled with a distinct parse state, which puts a finite upper-bound on the possible number of active processes and limits the size of the graph-structured stack. (In Figure 4.3, two processes, which were originally split off the process in state 4, merge into the process in state 3 by executing a goto action to the same state in U_3.)

The Reduce Action. A process executes a reduce action on a production p by following the chain of parent links down from its top-of-stack vertex v to the ancestor vertex from which the process began scanning for p earlier, essentially "popping" intervening vertices off its stack. Since merging means a vertex can have multiple parents, the reduce operation can lead back to multiple ancestors. When this happens, the process is again split into separate processes (one for each ancestor). (In Figure 4.3, the process in state 4 splits twice: first, when it encounters the two reduce actions, and again, when it encounters its two parents.) The ancestors will correspond to the set of vertices at a distance $\bar{p}$ from v, where $\bar{p}$ equals the number of symbols in the right-hand side of the pth production. Once reduced, a process shifts to the state s' indicated in the goto table for D_p (the nonterminal on the left-hand side of the pth production) given the state of the ancestor vertix. A process shifts on a nonterminal much as it does a terminal, with the exception that the new leaf is added to U_{i-1} rather than U_i. A process can only enter U_i by shifting on x_i.

The algorithm begins with a single initial process whose top-of-stack vertex is the root of the graph-structured stack. It then follows the general procedure outlined above for each symbol in the input string, continuing until there are either no leaves added to U_i (i.e., no more active processes), which denotes *rejection*, or a process executes the accept action on scanning the $n + 1$st input symbol '⊣,' which denotes *acceptance*.

4.3. Analysis of Tomita's Algorithm

In this section, Tomita's algorithm is presented formally as a recognizer for input string $x_1 \cdots x_n$. This definition is understood to be with respect to an extended LR parse table with start state S_0 constructed from a CF grammar G.

4.3.1. Definitions

The productions of G are numbered arbitrarily $1, \cdots, d$. Each production has the form

$$D_p \rightarrow C_{p1} \cdots C_{p\bar{p}} \quad (1 \le p \le d)$$

where $\bar{p}$ is the number of symbols on the right-hand side of the pth production.

The entries of the extended LR parse table are accessed with the functions ACTIONS and GOTO.

- ACTIONS(s,x) returns a set of actions from the action table along the row of state s under the column labeled x. This set will contain no more than one of a shift action shs' *or* an accept action acc; it may contain any number of reduce actions re$p$. An empty action set corresponds to an error.
- GOTO(s,D_p) returns a state s' from the goto table along the row of state go$s$ under the column labeled with nonterminal D_p.

Each *vertex* of the graph-structured stack is a triple $\langle i, s, l \rangle$, where i is an integer corresponding to the ith input symbol scanned (at which point the vertex was created as a leaf), s is a parse state (corresponding to a row of the parse table), and l is a set of parent vertices. The processes described in the last section are represented implicitly by the vertices in successive U_i's. The root of the graph-structured stack, and hence the initial process, is the vertex $\langle 0, S_0, \emptyset \rangle$.

4.3.2. The Recognizer

The recognizer is a function of one argument REC($x_1 \cdots x_n$). It calls upon the functions SHIFT(v,s) and REDUCE(v,p). SHIFT(v,s) either (1) adds a new leaf to U_i labeled with parse state s whose parent is vertex v or (2) merges vertex v with the parents of an existing leaf. REDUCE(v,p) executes a reduce action from vertex v using production p. REDUCE calls upon the function

ANCESTORS($v,\bar{p}$), which returns the set of all ancestor vertices a distance of $\bar{p}$ from vertex v. These functions, which vary somewhat from the formal definition given in Tomita (1985),[2] are defined in Figure 4.4.

In REC, [1] adds the end-of-sentence symbol ' $\vdash$ ' to the end of the input string; [2] initializes the root of the graph-structured stack; [3] iterates through the symbols of the input string. On each symbol x_i, [4] processes the vertices (denoting the active processes) of successive U_{i-1}'s, adding each vertex to P to signify that it has been processed. On each vertex v, [5] executes the shift, reduce, and accept actions from the action table according to v's state s. After processing the vertices in U_{i-1}, [6] checks whether a vertex was added to U_i, ensuring that at least one process is still active before scanning x_{i+1}.

In SHIFT, [7] shifts a process into state s by adding a vertex to U_i labeled s. If a vertex labeled s already exists, v is added to its parents, merging processes; otherwise, a new vertex is created with a single parent v.

In REDUCE, [8] iterates through the ancestor vertices a distance of $\bar{p}$ from v, setting s'' to the state indicated in the goto table under D_p given the ancestor's state s'. Each ancestor vertex v_1' is shifted into U_{i-1} on s''. [9] checks whether such a vertex v'' already exists. (If not, [14] adds a vertex labeled s'' to U_{i-1}.) If v'' does already exist, [10] checks that a shift from the current ancestor v_1' has not already been made. (If it has, then some segment of the input string has been recognized as an instance of the same nonterminal D_p in two different ways, and the current derivation can be discarded as ambiguous; otherwise, v_1' is merged with the parents of the existing vertex.) Before merging, [11] checks whether v_1' is a "clone" vertex, created by [13] in an earlier call to REDUCE (as described below). If v_1' is not a clone, [12] adds it to the parents of v'', merging processes. [13] checks if v'' has already been processed. If so, then it missed any reductions through v_1'. To correct this, v'' is "cloned" into v_c'' (i.e., a variant on v'' with a single parent v_1'), and all reduce actions executed on v'' are now executed on v_c''.

Returning to [11], when reducing on a null production, ANCESTORS will return a clone vertex as the ancestor of itself. If a variant v_2' of v_1' already exists in the parents of v'', then v_1' is a clone of v_2'. At this point v'' has already been processed, meaning that there could still be reductions that have not gone through the single parent of v_1'. To correct this, v'' is again cloned, and all reduce actions executed on v'' are executed on the new clone v_c''.

Finally, in ANCESTORS, [15] recursively descends the chain of parents of vertex v, returning the set of vertices a distance of k from v.

---

2. Tomita's functions REDUCE and REDUCE-E have been collapsed into a single REDUCE function; also added were the ANCESTORS function and the concept of a "clone" vertex. While these changes do not alter Tomita's algorithm significantly, they were helpful in developing ideas about its complexity.

```
        REC (x_1 ··· x_n)
[1]        let x_{n+1} := ⊣
           let U_i := [ ]    (0 ≤ i ≤ n)
[2]        let U_0 := [⟨0, S_0, ∅⟩]
[3]        for i from 1 to n+1
              let P := [ ]
[4]           for ∀v = ⟨i-1, s, l⟩ s.t. v ∈ U_{i-1}
                 let P := P ∘ [v]
[5]              if ∃'sh s'' ∈ ACTIONS (s, x_i), SHIFT (v, s')
                 for ∀'re p' ∈ ACTIONS (s, x_i), REDUCE (v, p)
                 if 'acc' ∈ ACTIONS (s, x_i), accept
[6]           if U_i is empty, reject


        SHIFT (v, s)
[7]        if ∃v' = ⟨i, s, l⟩ s.t. v' ∈ U_i
              let l := l ∪ {v}
           else
              let U_i := U_i ∘ [⟨i, s, {v}⟩]


        REDUCE (v, p)
[8]        for ∀v_1' = ⟨j', s', l_1'⟩ s.t. v_1' ∈ ANCESTORS (v, p̄)
              let 'go s''' := GOTO (s', D_p)
[9]           if ∃v'' = ⟨i-1, s'', l''⟩ s.t. v'' ∈ U_{i-1}
[10]             if v_1' ∈ l''
                    do nothing (ambiguous)
                 else
[11]                if ∃v_2' = ⟨j', s', l_2'⟩ s.t. v_2' ∈ l''
                       let v_c'' := ⟨i-1, s'', {v_1'}⟩
                       for ∀'re p' ∈ ACTIONS (s'', x_i), REDUCE (v_c'', p)
                    else
[12]                   let l'' := l'' ∪ {v_1'}
[13]             if v'' ∈ P
                    let v_c'' := ⟨i-1, s'', {v_1'}⟩
                    for ∀'re p' ∈ ACTIONS (s'', x_i), REDUCE (v_c'', p)
              else
[14]             let U_{i-1} := U_{i-1} ∘ [⟨i-1, s'', {v_1'}⟩]


        ANCESTORS (v = ⟨j, s, l⟩, k)
[15]       if k = 0
              return ({v})
           else
              return (⋃_{v'∈l} ANCESTORS (v', k - 1))
```

Figure 4.4. Tomita's algorithm

4.3.3. The General-Case Time Bound

Tomita's algorithm is an $O(n^{\bar{p}+1})$ recognizer in general, where $\bar{p}$ is the greatest $\bar{p}$ in G. The reasons for this are as follows:

a. Since each vertex in U_i must be labeled with a distinct parse state, the number of vertices in any U_i is bounded by the number of parse states;

b. The number of parents l of a vertex $v = \langle i, s, l \rangle$ in U_i is proportional to i. Because processes could have begun scanning for some production p in each U_j ($j \leq i$), a process in U_i could reduce using p and split into $\sim i$ processes (one for each ancestor in a distinct U_j). Then each process could shift on D_p to the same state in U_i and, thus, that vertex could have $\sim i$ parents;

c. For each x_{i+1}, SHIFT will be called a bounded number of times (at most once for each vertex in U_i). SHIFT executes in a bounded number of steps.

d. For each x_{i+1} and production p, REDUCE(v,p) will be called a bounded number of times in REC, and REDUCE(v_c'',p) (the recursive call to REDUCE) will be called no more than $\sim i$ times. The reason for the former is the same as in (c). The latter is due to the conditions on the recursive call, which maintain that it can be called no more than once for each parent of a vertex in U_i, of which there are at most proportional to i;

e. REDUCE(v,p), because at most $\sim i$ vertices can be returned by ANCESTORS, executes in $\sim i$ steps plus the steps needed to execute ANCESTORS.

f. ANCESTORS(v,$\bar{p}$) executes in $\sim i^{\bar{p}}$ steps in the worst case. While at most $\sim i$ processes could have begun scanning for p, the number of paths by which any single process could reach v in U_i is bounded by the number of ways the intervening input symbols can be partitioned among the $\bar{p}$ vocabulary symbols in the right-hand side of production p. For a process that started from U_j ($j \leq i$), the number of paths to v in U_i in the recognition of p can be proportional to

$$\sum_{m_1=j}^{0} \sum_{m_2=m_1}^{0} \cdots \sum_{m_{\bar{p}-1}=m_{\bar{p}-2}}^{0} 1.$$

Summing from $j = 0, \cdots, i$ gives a closed form proportional to $i^{\bar{p}}$. ANCESTORS(v_c'',$\bar{p}$), where $v_c'' = \langle i, s, \{v'\} \rangle$, executes in $\sim i^{\bar{p}-1}$ steps because there is that many ways $\sim i$ ancestor vertices could reach v' and only one way v' could reach v_c'';

g. The worst case time bound is dominated by the time spent in ANCESTORS, which can be added to the time spent in REDUCE. Since REDUCE(v,p), with a bound $\sim i^{\bar{p}}$, is called only a bounded number of times, and REDUCE(v_c'',p), with a time bound of $\sim i^{\bar{p}-1}$, is called at most $\sim i$ times, the worst case time to process any x_i is $\sim i^{\bar{p}}$, for each $i = 0, \cdots, n+1$ and longest production ρ;

h. Summing from $i = 0, \cdots, n+1$ gives REC a general time bound proportional to $n^{\bar{p}+1}$.

As a result, this time bound indicates that Tomita's algorithm only belongs to complexity class $O(n^3)$ when applied to grammars in Chomsky normal form (CNF)[3] or some other equally truncated notation.

---

3. In CNF, productions can have one of two forms, A → BC or A → a; thus, the length of the longest production is at most 2.

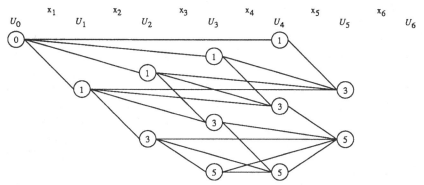

Figure 4.5. Worst-case graph-structured stack.

4.4. Modifying Tomita's Algorithm for N^3 Time

In this section, Tomita's algorithm is made an $O(n^3)$ recognizer for CF grammars with productions of arbitrary length. Essentially, the modifications are to the ANCESTORS function. ANCESTORS is the only function that forces us to use i^p steps. It is interesting to note that ANCESTORS can take this many steps even though (1) it returns at most $\sim i$ ancestor vertices and (2) there are at most $\sim i$ intervening vertices and edges between a vertex in U_i and its ancestors. This indicates that ANCESTORS can recurse down the same subpaths more than once. The efficiency of ANCESTORS and Tomita's algorithm can be improved by eliminating this redundancy.

4.4.1. Following Redundant Paths

The redundancy in the ANCESTORS function becomes apparent when considering the graph-structured stack shown in Figure 4.5. This is a continuation of the example presented earlier in Section 4.2. The parser is scanning x_6 and has two active process in states 3 and 5.

In fact, for each U_i ($3 \leq i \leq n$), there will always be processes in states 3 and 5, and both processes will always have proportional to i parents. Further, the parents of the process in state 5 will consist of all processes in states 3 and 5 in each U_j, for j from 0 to $i - 1$. As a result, to reduce using production 1 (length three) from a process in state 5 in U_i, ANCESTORS will traverse $\sim i^3$ paths. Since there are at most $\sim i$ distinct vertices that ANCESTORS can return, it must be traversing tails of the same subpaths more than once.

4.4.2. The Ancestors Table

The redundancy in ANCESTORS can be avoided by treating it as a table look-up function. Assume there is a two-dimensional "ancestors" table. One dimension is indexed on the vertices in the graph-structured stack, and the other is indexed on integers $k = 1, \cdots, \bar{p}$, where $\bar{p}$ equals the greatest $\bar{p}$. Each entry (v, k) is the set of ancestor vertices a distance of k from vertex v. Then, ANCESTORS(v,k) returns the (at most) $\sim i$ ancestor at (v, k) in ~ 1 steps. Of course, the table must be filled dynamically during the recognition process, so the time expended in this task must also be determined.

In the modified algorithm, ANCESTORS is defined as a table look-up function that dynamically generates table entries the first time they are requested. In this definition, the ancestor table is represented by changing the parent field l of a vertex $v = \langle i, s, l \rangle$ from a set of parent vertices to an ancestor field a. For a vertex $v = \langle i, s, a \rangle$, a consists of a set of tuples $\langle k, l_k \rangle$, such that l_k is the set of ancestor vertices a distance of k from v.

4.4.3. Modifying the Recognizer

Figure 4.6 shows the necessary modifications made to the definitions of Figure 4.4; the function REC is unchanged. In SHIFT, [1] adds a vertex to U_i labeled s. If such a vertex does not already exist, one is created whose ancestor field records that v is the ancestor vertex at a distance of 1; otherwise, v is added to the other distance-1 ancestors.

In REDUCE, [2] iterates through the ancestor vertices a distance of $\bar{p}$ from v, setting s'' to the state indicated in the goto table under D_p given the ancestor's state s'. Each ancestor vertex v_1' is shifted into U_{i-1} on s''. [3] checks whether such a vertex v'' already exists. (If not, [10] will add a vertex labeled s'' to U_{i-1}.) If v'' does already exist, [4] checks that a shift from the current ancestor v_1' has not already been made. If it has, then v_1' can be discarded as ambiguous; if not, then v_1' can be merged with the other ancestors a distance of 1 from v''. Before merging, [5] checks whether v_1' is a clone vertex as described in Section 4.2. If v_1' is a clone (the result of being reduced on a null production), v'' is again cloned, and all reduce actions executed on v'' are executed on the new clone v_c''. After the application of REDUCE, [6] updates the ancestor table stored in v'' to record entries made in the ancestor field a_c'' of the clone when $k \geq 2$. Otherwise, if v_1' is not a clone, [7] adds it to the distance-1 ancestors of v'', merging processes. [8] checks if v'' has already been processed. If so, then it missed any reductions through v_1', so v'' is cloned into v_c'' and all reduce actions executed on v'' are now executed on v_c''. After reducing v_c'', [9] updates the ancestor table stored in v'' to record entries made in the ancestor field a_c'' of the clone when $k \geq 2$.

In ANCESTORS, [11] searches a (the portion of the ancestor table stored with v) for ancestor vertices at a distance of k from v. If an entry exists, those vertices are returned; if not, [12] calls ANCESTORS recursively to generated those vertices and, before returning the generated vertices, records them in the ancestor field of v.

```
     SHIFT (v, s)
[1]     if ∃v' = ⟨i, s, a⟩ s.t. v' ∈ U_i ∧ ⟨1, l⟩ ∈ a,
           let l := l ∪ {v}
        else
           let U_i := U_i ∘ [⟨i, s, [⟨1, {v}⟩]⟩]


     REDUCE (v, p)
[2]     for ∀v_1' = ⟨j', s', a_1'⟩ s.t. v_1' ∈ ANCESTORS (v, p̄)
           let `go s''` := GOTO (s', D_p)
[3]        if ∃v'' = ⟨i − 1, s'', a''⟩ s.t. v'' ∈ U_{i−1} ∧ ⟨1, l''⟩ ∈ a''
[4]           if v_1' ∈ l''
                 do nothing (ambiguous)
              else
[5]           if ∃v_2' = ⟨j', s', a_2'⟩ s.t. v_2' ∈ l''
                 let v_c'' := ⟨i − 1, s'', a_c''⟩ s.t. a_c'' = [⟨1, {v_1'}⟩]
                 for ∀`re p' ∈ ACTIONS (s'', x_i), REDUCE (v_c'', p)
[6]              let l_{k_1} := l_{k_1} ∪ l_{k_2} s.t. ⟨k, l_{k_1}⟩ ∈ a'' ∧ ⟨k, l_{k_2}⟩
                    ∈ a_c'' (k≥2)
              else
[7]           let l'' := l'' ∪ {v_1'}
[8]           if v'' ∈ P
                 let v_c'' := ⟨i − 1, s'', a_c''⟩ s.t. a_c'' = [⟨1, {v_1'}⟩]
                 for ∀`re p' ∈ ACTIONS (s'', x_i), REDUCE (v_c'', p)
[9]              let l_{k_1} := l_{k_1} ∪ l_{k_2} s.t. ⟨k, l_{k_1}⟩ ∈ a'' ∧ ⟨k, l_{k_2}⟩
                    ∈ a_c'' (k≥2)
           else
[10]         let U_{i−1} := U_{i−1} ∘ [⟨i − 1, s'', {v_1'}⟩]


     ANCESTORS (v = ⟨j, s, a⟩, k)
[11]    if k = 0,
           return ({v})
        else
        if ∃⟨k, l_k⟩ ∈ a,
           return (l_k)
        else
[12]       let l_k := ⋃_{v'∈l_1|⟨1,l_1⟩∈a} ANCESTORS (v', k − 1)
           let a := a ∪ {⟨k, l_k⟩}
           return (l_k)
```

Figure 4.6. Modified algorithm

4.4.4. The General-Case Time Bound

The question now becomes how much time is spent filling the ancestor table. For ANCESTORS$(v, \bar{p})$, time is bounded in the worst case by $\sim i^2$ steps, while for ANCESTORS$(v_c'', \bar{p})$, it is bounded by $\sim i$ steps.

In general, ANCESTORS(v,k), where $v = \langle i, s, a \rangle$, will take $\sim i$ steps to execute the first time it is called (one for each recursive call to ANCESTORS($v',k-1$), where $v' \in l_1$ and $\langle 1, l_1 \rangle \in a$) and ~ 1 steps thereafter. When ANCESTORS($v,\bar{p}$) is executed, there are $\sim i$ such "virgin" vertices between v and its ancestors, and so this call can execute $\sim i^2$ steps in the worst case. ANCESTORS($v_c'',\bar{p}$) is called only after the call to ANCESTORS($v,\bar{p}$) has been made, where v_c'' is a clone of v. This means that $\sim i$ of the vertices between v' and the ancestor vertices have been processed, so the call to ANCESTORS($v',\bar{p}-1$) could take at most proportional to i steps for each of a bounded number of intervening vertices.

Given this, the upper bound on the number of steps that can be executed by the total calls on REDUCE for a given x_i is proportional to i^2. Summing from $i = 0, \cdots, n+1$ gives $\sim n^3$ steps as the worst-case upper bound on the execution time of the modified algorithm.

4.4.5. Space Complexity

The modified algorithm introduced above achieves an $O(n^3)$ time bound by making a trade off between time and space. To ensure that this trade off is not disproportionate, it is important to compare the space complexity of both algorithms. In doing so, we find that the space complexity is impaired by at most a constant factor.

The space complexity of Tomita's algorithm, as it appears in Section 4.3, is proportional to n^2 in the worst case. This is because the space requirements of the algorithm are dominated by the requirements of the graph-structured stack. There are a bounded number of vertices in each U_i of the graph-structured stack, and each vertex can have at most $\sim i$ parents. Summing again from $i = 0, \cdots, n+1$ gives $\sim n^2$ as the worst-case space requirement for the graph-structured stack.

In the modified algorithm, the space requirements of the graph-structured stack are increased by at most a constant factor of n^2. This is because the modification replaces the $\sim i$ parents of a vertex in U_i with at most $\sim \bar{p}i$ entries in the ancestors field. So, for a vertex $v = \langle i, s, a \rangle$ s.t. $v \in U_i$, the ancestors field a will be a subset of $\{ \langle c, l_c \rangle | 1 \le c \le \bar{p} \}$ where $|l_c| \simeq i$. Summing from $i = 0, \cdots, n+1$ gives $\sim \bar{p}n^2$ or $\sim n^2$ still as a worst case upper bound on space.

4.5. Empirical Results

The variation on Tomita's algorithm presented in Section 4.3 and the modified algorithm presented in Section 4.4 have both been implemented in C. The graphs in Figures 4.7 and 4.8 show empirical results comparing the time and space requirements of both implementations. Each time/space graph set corresponds

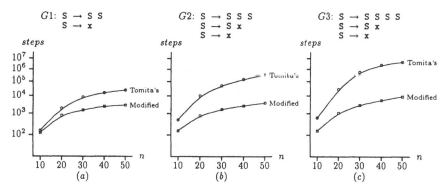

Figure 4.7. Comparison of execution steps.

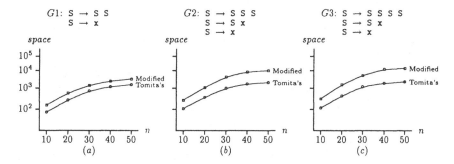

Figure 4.8. Comparison of space requirements.

to the grammars, $G1$, $G2$, and $G3$, which are dominated by productions of length two, three, and four, respectively.

4.5.1. Comparing Execution Steps

The time graphs in Figure 4.7 measure the number of calls to SHIFT, REDUCE, and ANCESTORS. The input consists of strings of x's varying in length from 10 to 50.

Our analysis of time complexity predicts that the modified algorithm will take roughly the same number of steps for each grammar, while the steps taken by Tomita's algorithm will increase as a function of the length of the dominant production. The empirical data gathered from our two implementations agrees with this prediction. When $n = 50$, the modified algorithm took approximately 7000 steps for grammar $G1$ in Figure 4.7 (*a*), 6000 for $G2$ in Figure 4.7 (*b*), and 10,000 for $G3$ in Figure 4.7 (*c*); Tomita's algorithm took approximately 44,000 steps for grammar $G1$, 660,000 for $G2$, and 7,300,000 for $G3$.

Table 4.1. *Comparison of space requirements*

		10	20	30	40	50
G1	Tomita's	91	381	871	1561	2451
	Modified	218	838	1858	3278	5098
	Factor Δ	2.4	2.2	2.1	2.1	2.1
G2	Tomita's	119	534	1249	2264	3579
	Modified	421	2001	4781	8761	13941
	Factor Δ	3.5	3.7	3.8	3.9	3.9
G3	Tomita's	140	670	1600	2930	4660
	Modified	522	2832	7162	13492	21822
	Factor Δ	3.6	4.2	4.5	4.6	4.6

4.5.2. Comparing Space Requirements

Table 4.1 compares the number of edges required by the graph-structured stack (in Tomita's algorithm) and the length of entries in the ancestors table (in the modified algorithm).

The number of vertices required is the same for both algorithms and is not counted; space that can be reclaimed before scanning successive x_i's is also not counted. This comparison is shown graphically in Figure 4.8.

Our analysis of space complexity predicts that Tomita's algorithm will require $\sim n^2$ space and that the modified algorithm will require at most a factor of n^2 additional space. The empirical evidence also agrees with this prediction. The space requirements of the modified algorithm differs from Tomita's algorithm by a factor of ~ 2.1 for grammar $G1$ in Figure 4.8 (a), ~ 3.9 for $G2$ in Figure 4.8 (b), and ~ 4.7 for $G3$ in Figure 4.8 (c).

4.6. Less Than N^3 Time

Several of the better known general CF algorithms have been shown to run in less than $O(n^3)$ time for certain subclasses of grammars. Therefore, it is of interest to ask if Tomita's algorithm, as well as the modified version presented here, can also recognize some subclasses of CF grammars in less than $O(n^3)$ time. In this section, I informally describe two such subclasses that can be recognized in $O(n^2)$ and $O(n)$ time, respectively. The arguments for their existence parallel those given by Earley (1968), where they are formally specified.

4.6.1. Time $O(n^2)$ Grammars

ANCESTORS is the only function that forces us to use $\sim i^p$ steps in Tomita's algorithm and $\sim i^2$ steps in the modified algorithm. We determined that this can happen when there exists more than one path from the reducing vertex v in U_i to an ancestor vertex v' in U_j $(j \leq i)$, i.e., when the symbols $x_j \cdots x_i$ are derived from a nonterminal D_p in more than one way, indicating that grammar G is ambiguous.

If G is unambiguous, then there will be at most one path from a given v' to v. This means that the bounded calls to ANCESTORS($v,\bar{p}$) can take at most $\sim i$ steps and that ANCESTORS($v_c'',\bar{p}$) can take at most a bounded number of steps. The first observation is due to the fact that there are $\sim i$ ancestor vertices that can be reached in only one way. Similarly, the second observation is due to the fact that if ANCESTORS($v_c'',\bar{p}$) took $\sim i$ steps, returning $\sim i$ ancestors, and was called $\sim i$ times, then some ancestor vertices must have shifted into U_i in more than one way, proving by contradiction that grammar G is not unambiguous.

So, if the grammar is unambiguous, then the total time spent in REDUCE for any x_i is $\sim i$ and the worst case time bound for the Tomita's algorithm is $O(n^2)$. A similar result is true for the modified algorithm.

4.6.2. Time $O(n)$ Grammars

In his thesis, Earley (1968) points out that " *... for some grammars the number of states in a state set can grow indefinitely with the length of the string being recognized. For some others there is a fixed bound on the size of any state set. We call the latter grammars bounded state grammars.*" While Earley's "states" have a different meaning than states in Tomita's algorithm, a similar phenomena occurs, i.e., for the bounded state grammars there is a fixed bound on the number of parents any vertex can have.

In Tomita's algorithm, bounded state grammars can be recognized in time $O(n)$ for the following reason. No vertex can have more than a bounded number of ancestors. Otherwise, $\sim i$ vertices could be added to the parents of some vertex in U_i, proving by contradiction that the grammar is not bounded state. This means that the ANCESTORS function can execute in a bounded number of steps. Likewise, REDUCE can only be called a bounded number of times. Summing over the x_i gives us an upper bound $\sim n$. Again, a similar result is true for the modified algorithm.

Interestingly enough, Earley states that almost all LR(k) grammars are bounded state, as well, which suggests that Tomita's algorithm, given k-symbol look ahead, should perform with little loss of efficiency as compared to a standard LR(k) algorithm when the grammar is "close" to LR(k). Earley also points out that not all bounded state grammars are unambiguous; thus, there are non-LR(k) grammars for which Tomita's algorithm can perform with LR(k) efficiency.

4.7. Concluding Remarks

The results in this chapter support in part Tomita's claim (1985) of efficiency for his algorithm. These results also give support to his claim that his algorithm should run with near LR(k) efficiency for near LR(k) grammars.

Tomita's algorithm is shown to be in the same complexity class as existing general CF algorithms when the length of the longest production is no greater than two, such as CNF grammars. Although any CF grammar can be automatically converted to CNF (Hopcraft and Ullman, 1979), this is not necessarily a desirable approach to take for practical parsing. The extended parse table constructed from grammar converted to CNF will contain a greater number of reduce actions, as well as multiple action entries caused by increased shift/reduce and reduce/reduce conflicts. Further, derivation trees generated with the converted grammar must be modified to conform to the structure of the original grammar before code generation routines associated with the grammar can be applied.

Our modifications to Tomita's algorithm put it in this same complexity class with productions of arbitrary length. It should be noted, however, that this is likewise not a desirable adaptation for a practical parser. From a pragmatic perspective, the level of ambiguity for grammars and sentences in realistic applications is constrained by the fact that human readers must not be overwhelmed. Since, intuitively, human-readable grammars should never realize the worst-case $O(n^{\delta+1})$ time bound of Tomita's algorithm, the benefits of the ancestors table in the modified algorithm would not balance out its overhead cost.

The variation on Tomita's algorithm described in this chapter, as well as the modified algorithm, have been implemented in both LISP and C at The RAND Corporation. The LISP implementation (Kipps, 1988) is distributed with ROSIE (Kipps et al., 1987), a language for applications in artificial intelligence with a highly ambiguous English-like syntax. The C implementation is part of the RAND Translator-Generator project (Kipps, 1990), which is developing a "next generation" of YACC-like[4] translator-generator tools for non-LR(k) languages.

Acknowledgements

Elements of this work were originally supported by the Defense Advanced Research Projects Agency, under contract number MDA-903-85-C-0030. Additional support was provided as part of RAND Sponsored Research. For their efforts in securing this support, the author is indebted to Louis Miller, Iris Kameny, Ed Hall, Jed Marti, as well as others at RAND.

References

Aho, A. V., & Ullman, J. D., 1972, *The Theory of Parsing, Translation and Compiling*, Prentice-Hall, Englewood Cliffs, NJ.

---

4. YACC (Johnson, 1975) is a parser-generator for LALR(1) languages.

Chomsky, N., 1959, "On Certain Formal Properties of Grammars," in *Information and Control*, vol. 2, no. 2, pp. 137-167.

Earley, J., 1968, *An Efficient Context-Free Parsing Algorithm*, Ph.D. Thesis, Computer Science Dept., Carnegie-Mellon University, Pittsburg, PA.

Hopcraft, J. E., & Ullman, J. D., 1979, *Introduction to Automata Theory, Languages, and Computation*, Addison Wesley, Reading, MA.

Kipps, J. R., Florman, B., & Sowizral, H. A., 1987, *The New ROSIE Reference Manual and User's Guide*, R-3448-DARPA, The RAND Corporation.

Kipps, J. R., 1988, *A Table-Driven Approach to Fast Context-Free Parsing*, N-2841-DARPA, The RAND Corporation.

Kipps, J. R., 1990, *RACC: The RAND Compiler-Compiler, Reference Manual and User's Guide*, N-3100-RC, The RAND Corporation.

Knuth, D. E., 1965, "On the Translation of Languages from Left to Right," *Information and Control*, vol. 8, pp. 607-639.

Johnson, S. C., 1975, "YACC—Yet Another Compiler Compiler," CSTR 32, Bell Laboratories, Murray Hill, NJ.

Tomita, M., 1985, *An Efficient Context-Free Parsing Algorithm for Natural Languages and Its Applications*, Ph.D. Thesis, Computer Science Dept., Carnegie-Mellon University, Pittsburg, PA.

Younger, D. H., 1967, "Recognition and Parsing of Context-Free Languages in Time n^3," in *Information and Control*, vol. 10, no. 2, pp. 189-208.

5 GLR Parsing for ε-Grammers

Rahman Nozohoor-Farshi

5.1. Introduction

This chapter develops a modified version of Tomita's algorithm for parsing arbitrary context-free grammars with ε-productions. It also describes the parsing of cyclic grammars within the frame of this algorithm.

Tomita's GLR parsing algorithm, discussed in Chapter 1 and in detail in [9,10], is an efficient all-paths parsing method which is driven by an LR parse table with multi-valued entries. The parser employs an acyclic parse graph instead of the conventional LR parser stack. The parser starts as an ordinary LR parser, but splits up when multiple actions are encountered. Multiple parses are synchronized on their shift actions and are joined whenever they are found to be in the same state.

The parallel parsing of all possible paths makes Tomita's algorithm suitable for parsing nearly all the arbitrary context-free grammars. In fact, one may view his method as a precompiled form of Earley's algorithm [2,3]. Earley [2] proposed a form of precompiled approach to his method. However, his approach is limited to a restricted class of grammars, and in addition, the membership in this class is undecidable. Tomita's algorithm, on the other hand, is intended for use with general grammars. Since the method uses a parse table, it achieves a considerable efficiency over the Earley's non-compiled method which has to compute a set of LR items at each stage of parsing. In this respect, Tomita's algorithm can indeed be considered as a breakthrough in efficient parallel parsing in practical systems. However, there are some context-free grammars with ε-rules that cannot be handled by his original method properly. The problem causing cases involve cyclic and some non-cyclic grammars. Cyclic grammars have infinite ambiguity and therefore are usually excluded from syntactic analyses. The second group of the grammars consists of certain context-free grammars with ε-productions which some of them are unambiguous and others have bounded, bounded direct or unbounded degrees of ambiguity.

Grammars of the latter type may seldom be used to describe the syntax of natural language. In fact, an earlier paper [6] considers them as somewhat ill-designed. But, they may creep in easily when one is designing a natural language grammar with ε-rules. Such rules cause unexpected infinite loops in parsing. The goal of this chapter is to modify the parsing algorithm so that it can handle the second type grammars. However, it is shown that the new algorithm can handle the cyclic grammars as well if the infinite parse trees are encoded in a particular fashion.

The modification introduces cyclic subgraphs in the original graph-structured parse stack. These subgraphs correspond to the parsing of null substrings in the input sentence. Thus, the modification incurs no cost to the grammars or the inputs that do not need this feature. Therefore, this modification on Tomita's algorithm seems very desirable, specially that the new algorithm is now comparable to Earley's algorithm in its coverage, and yet it is in a precompiled form.

In the following sections, the two types of the grammars that cause problems in the original algorithm are discussed and the modified algorithm is presented.

5.2. Cyclic Grammars

Cyclic grammars are those in which a non-terminal, like A, can derive itself (i.e., $A \overset{+}{\Longrightarrow} A$). G_1 and G_2 are examples of cyclic grammars.

G_1:
  (1) $S \rightarrow A$
  (2) $A \rightarrow S$
  (3) $A \rightarrow x$

G_2:
  (1) $S \rightarrow S\,S$
  (2) $S \rightarrow x$
  (3) $S \rightarrow \varepsilon$

In G_1, $A \Longrightarrow S \Longrightarrow A$, and in G_2, $S \Longrightarrow S\,S \Longrightarrow S$. Cyclic grammars produce infinite number of parse trees for a finite length input such as "x" in $L(G_1)$ and $L(G_2)$. They cause problem in every parsing algorithm. Therefore, they have been avoided in describing the syntax of languages traditionally.

Both Earley's and Tomita's recognition algorithms will fail to detect the cyclicity of G_1 and G_2. Given an input sentence "x," however, it is accepted with respect to either grammar by Earley's algorithm and only with respect to G_1 by Tomita's algorithm. The second algorithm will not terminate when the grammar G_2 is used. Furthermore, it is shown in [9,10] that Earley's tree constructing algorithm will also encounter inconsistency problems in this case. Tomita [9] discusses the cyclic grammars and rules out their inclusion in natural language parsing. Such exclusion can be achieved through a simple test before generating a parse table (see [1] for example).

5.3. Non-cyclic Grammars

Among the non-cyclic grammars that cannot be handled by the original algorithm are the examples G_3, G_4, G_5 and G_6 below.

G_3:
  (1) $S \rightarrow A\,S\,b$
  (2) $S \rightarrow x$
  (3) $A \rightarrow \varepsilon$

G_5:
  (1) $S \rightarrow A\,S\,b$
  (2) $S \rightarrow x$
  (3) $A \rightarrow t$
  (4) $A \rightarrow \varepsilon$

G_4: G_6:
  (1) $S \to M$ (1) $S \to M\ N$
  (2) $S \to N$ (2) $M \to A\ M\ b$
  (3) $M \to A\ M\ b$ (3) $M \to x$
  (4) $M \to x$ (4) $N \to b\ N\ A$
  (5) $N \to A\ N\ b$ (5) $N \to x$
  (6) $N \to x$ (6) $A \to \varepsilon$
  (7) $A \to \varepsilon$

G_3 is unambiguous, G_4 has bounded ambiguity, G_5 has bounded direct ambiguity while G_6 has unbounded ambiguity. The following gives the definitions of these terms.

Definition: A context-free grammar G has bounded ambiguity of degree k if each sentence in $L(G)$ has at most k distinct derivation trees. G_4 has bounded ambiguity of degree 2.

Definition: A context-free grammar G has unbounded ambiguity if for each $i \geq 1$, there exists a sentence in $L(G)$ which has at least i distinct derivation trees.

Definition: The degree of direct ambiguity of a non-terminal A with respect to a string x is the number of distinct tuples $(p, x_1, x_2, \ldots, x_n)$, where p is a production $A \to B_1 B_2 \cdots B_n$, and $x_1 x_2 \cdots x_n = x$ is a factorization of x such that $B_i \stackrel{*}{\Longrightarrow} x_i$ for $1 \leq n$.

Definition: A context-free grammar has bounded direct ambiguity of degree k if the degree of direct ambiguity of any of its non-terminals with respect to any string is at most k. The grammar G_5 has direct ambiguity of degree 2, in spite of being unboundedly ambiguous.

It is important to note that in the above examples, unlike cyclic grammars, there are only a finite number of parse trees for a given finite length input. A property common to these problem causing grammars is that there exists a non-terminal, say S, such that $S \stackrel{+}{\Longrightarrow} \alpha\ S\ \beta$ where $\alpha \stackrel{+}{\Longrightarrow} \varepsilon$ but $\beta \stackrel{*}{\not\Longrightarrow} \varepsilon$. For example, in G_3 or G_5, S can be rewritten as $S \Longrightarrow A\ S\ b \to S\ b$. The following algorithm decides whether a grammar has such property.

Algorithm: Identifying the ε-grammars that cannot be parsed by the original algorithm.

    Let $G = (N, T, P, S)$ be a context-free grammar with εproductions.

1. Compute the set of non-terminals $E = \{C | C \stackrel{+}{\Longrightarrow} \varepsilon$ that can derive a null string.
2. Let $\rho \subset N \times N$ be a binary relation such that $(A, B) \in \rho$ if and only if $A \to C_1 C_2 \cdots C_n B \alpha$ is a production in P and $C_i \in E$ for $1 \leq i \leq n$.
3. Let $\lambda \subset N \times N$ be a binary relation such that $(A, B) \in \gamma$ if and only if $A \to B \gamma$ is a production in P.
4. Compute the closure $R = (\lambda^* \rho \lambda^*)^+$. If there exists a non-terminal A where $(A, A) \in R$ then G cannot be parsed by the Tomita's original algorithm for ε-grammars.

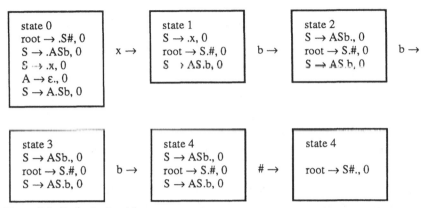

Figure 5.1. Earley's algorithm.

Obviously, as it is indicated from the above algorithm one may exclude the rules like those in the example grammars from Tomita's parsing algorithm. On the other hand, one may wish to keep or to add such rules in a grammar for the following reasons.

1. To capture some rare phenomena, for example, embedded that-sentences [[THAT [[THAT . . . [[THAT S] VP] . . .] VP]] VP] in which a number of terminal 'that's are omitted.

2. Grammars with ε-productions are more concise and readable than the grammars without ε-rules. In fact, elimination of ε-rules from a grammar may increase the size of the grammar exponentially. Therefore, one may use rules similar to the examples G_3 to G_6 to compact the grammar and the parse table, knowing that their presence should not affect the correct parsing of valid inputs. Furthermore, ε-rules play an important role in capturing natural language phenomenon like gaps in ellipsis and topicalization in many formalisms such as Generalized Phrase Structure Grammars.

3. More frequently, such rules may appear in a grammar when ε-productions are introduced without an adequate care. It is important to note that replacement of these rules (and their associated symbols) may not always be easy.

Grammars G_3 through G_6 can be parsed by Earley's algorithm with no problem. For example, consider the sentence xbbb $\in L(G_3)$. That algorithm will produce the states which are depicted in Figure 5.1.

However, these grammars cause an infinite loop in Tomita's algorithm. Applying the algorithm for ε-grammars (given in [9]) to the input sentence xbbb and the parse table for G_3 (Table 5.1), the result will be an infinite graph-structured stack as shown in Figure 5.2.

In Tomita's algorithm the state nodes created in the parse graph are partitioned into $U_0, U_1, \ldots, U_n$ where each U_i is the set of state vertices which are created before the shifting of the word a_{i+1} in the input. Furthermore, in the presence of ε-productions, each U_i is partitioned into $U_{i,0}, U_{i,1}, U_{i,2}, \ldots$. Each $U_{i,j}$ denotes the set of state vertices created while parsing the j-th null construct after the i-th

Table 5.1. *Parse table for* G_3

State	x	b	#	A	S
0	re3,sh3			2	1
1			acc		
2	re3,sh3			2	4
3		re2	re2		
4		sh5			
5		re1	re1		
	Action table			*Goto table*	

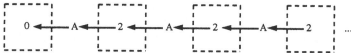

Figure 5.2. Tomita's algorithm.

input symbol a_i is shifted and before the shifting of the next actual input symbol a_{i+1} takes place. Tomita assumes that the number of null constituents between every adjacent pair of input symbols is always finite. Though his assumption is correct for non-cyclic grammars, it cannot be incorporated as such in the parser since it will require arbitrary and complex lookaheads in general case. As it was noted earlier this strategy fails in the example grammars.

It is interesting to note that the same strategy will succeed in the case of LR grammar G_3^r which is the reverse of G_3.

G_3^r:
    (1) $S \to b\ S\ A$
    (2) $S \to x$
    (3) $A \to \varepsilon$

The difference between G_3 and G_3^r is that in G_3 a null deriving constituent appears on the left part of a recursive phrase, while in G_3^r, it appears on the right side of the recursive construct. Thus, the parser for G_3 does not know how many A's it has to create before consuming the first input word "x." In the case of G_3^r, the left context provides enough information to limit the number of empty constructs to a finite size.

One may observe that though G_3 is an unambiguous grammar, it is not LR(k) for any k. Viewing differently, one may argue that such grammars can be parsed deterministically and more efficiently by non-canonical parsers. Marcus' parser [5] and bottom-up variations of it described in [7,8] can handle this grammar in a much better way, since they create the rightmost A in the parse tree first. The reader may also consult [7,8] to see the advantage of these parsers over Tomita's algorithm when grammars like G_7 are to be parsed.

G_7:
    (1) $S \rightarrow a\, S\, a$
    (2) $S \rightarrow B\, S\, b$
    (3) $S \rightarrow C\, S\, c$
    (4) $B \rightarrow a$
    (5) $C \rightarrow a$
    (6) $S \rightarrow x$

However, it should be emphasized that the whole thrust and the advantage of Tomita's parser are in obtaining multiple parses with respect to ambiguous grammars such as those in the examples G_4 to G_6.

5.4. Modified Algorithm

This section modifies Tomita's algorithm so that the second type grammars can be handled within its framework. It is believed that this modification introduces a precompiled algorithm which is equivalent to Earley's parser and can be applied to all the arbitrary context-free grammars.

To accommodate grammars like G_3 to G_6 within Tomita's parsing method cycles will be allowed in the graph-structured parse stack. These cycles are introduced in the parse graph in a very restricted way. Each cyclic subgraph represents a regular expression that corresponds to parsing of a null substring between two adjacent input symbols. Here, unlike Tomita's algorithm for ε-grammars [9], each U_i is not partitioned any further. So, the set of state vertices of each cyclic subgraph entirely lies within a single U_i. Obviously, cycles are created within U_i only if parsing of the input sentence requires them. Since the parse graph is cyclic now the reductions are performed along arbitrary paths (i.e., paths that are not simple and may contain repetitive vertices or arcs). Such paths are usually termed *(directed) walks* in graph theory.

Although this approach is intuitive but it has its roots in LR theory. In LR parsing, the finite automaton (from which a parse table is extracted) represents the set of all viable prefixes of the grammar in closed form. The parse stack, on the other hand, represents an actual viable prefix (of a right sentential form) in open form. The actual viable prefix is built from the input symbols which are consumed by the LR parser. It is necessary to hold the actual viable prefix in the stack so that the parser can be provided with the exact left context. However, in the modified all-paths parser there is no need to keep the null-deriving segments of the left context in open form. For example, in parsing sentences like $xb\ldots b \in L(G_3)$, ε and $A\ldots A$ are the viable prefixes when the parser scans the first input symbol "x." Each A derives a null string and it is not known exactly how many of them should be assumed. To avoid building infinite number of possibilities the left context is represented in the closed form $\varepsilon + AA^*$. The parser will pick as many A's as it needs from this regular expression when the remainder of the sentence

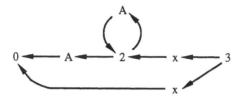

Figure 5.3. Snapshot of parse graph when "x" is just shifted.

Table 5.2. *Parse table for grammer G_5.*

State	t	x	b	#	A	S
0	sh4,re4	sh3,re4			2	1
1			acc			
2	sh4,re4	sh3,re4			2	5
3			re2	re2		
4	re3	re3				
5			sh6			
6			re1	re1		
		Action table			*Goto table*	

is seen. The snapshot of the parse graph when "x" is just shifted appears in Figure 5.3.

Similarly, consider the example grammar G_5. The parse table for this grammar is shown in Table 5.2. Figure 5.4 depicts the snapshot of the parse graph after the parser consumed the prefix txb of the sentence $txb...b$, and all the appropriate reductions were done.

In this example, the left context just before shifting the word "x" can be represented as the regular expression $(AA^* A + A)A^*$. For clarity, the bold faced **A** represents the non-terminal obtained by reducing "t." For the same reason, the combining of the identical symbol vertices which are adjacent to a same state vertex, (a measure of optimization suggested in [9,10]), is avoided in the illustrated examples and in the algorithm that to follow.

Another interesting example is the grammar G_8.

G_8:
    (1) $S \rightarrow x$
    (2) $S \rightarrow B S b$
    (3) $S \rightarrow A S b$
    (4) $B \rightarrow A A$
    (5) $A \rightarrow \varepsilon$

The parse table for this grammar is Table 5.3. An interested reader using this table may verify that U_0 in this case will have the format shown in Figure 5.5.

In the above examples, an LALR(1) parser generator, similar to YACC [4],

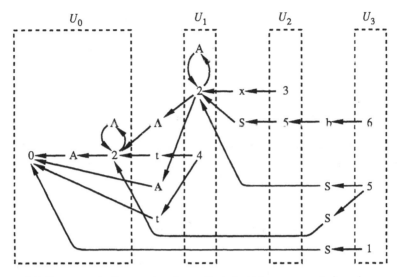

Figure 5.4. Parse graph after parsing the prefix txb of the sentence $txb \ldots b$.

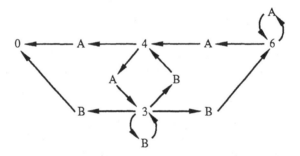

Figure 5.5. U_0 for the grammer in Table 5.3.

is used to obtain the parse tables with multi-valued entries. Tomita [9,10] also uses LALR(1) tables, however, using non-optimized LR(1) tables will decrease the number of superfluous reductions in general.

The following is a description of the modified algorithm. For simplicity, the algorithm is given in the form of a recognizer rather than a parser. The recognizer can be augmented in a way similar to that of [9] to provide a parser that also creates the parse forest. The notation used here is very similar to that in [9], except that the routine responsible for performing the reductions, like Earley [2,3], is now called COMPLETER. The algorithm appends an end marker # to the input sentence, i.e., $a_{n+1} = \#$.

Table 5.3. *Parse table for grammer G_8*

State	x	b	#	A	B	S
0	sh2,re5			4	3	1
1			acc			
2		re1	re1			
3	sh2,re5			4	3	5
4	sh2,re5			6	3	7
5		sh8				
6	sh2,re4,re5			6	3	7
7		sh9				
8		re2	re2			
9		re3	re3			
	Action table			*Goto table*		

Recognition Algorithm:

Variables

Γ: The parse graph.

U_i: The set of state vertices created just before shifting the input worda_{i+1}.

s_0:   The initial state of the parser.

A: The set of active nodes on which the parser will act.

Q: The set of shift operations to be carried out.

R: The set of reduction to be performed.

PARSE$(G, a_1 \ldots a_n)$

- $\Gamma := \emptyset$.
- $a_{n+1} := \#$.
- $r := \text{FALSE}$.
- Create a vertex v_0 labeled s_0 in Γ.
- $U_0 := \{v_0\}$.
- For $i := 0$ to n do PARSEWORD (i).
- Return r.

PARSEWORD(i)

- $A := U_i$.
- $R := \emptyset; \; Q := \emptyset$.
- Repeat
    if $A \neq \emptyset$ then do ACTOR
    else if $R \neq \emptyset$ then do COMPLETER
  until $R = \emptyset$ and $A = \emptyset$.
- Do SHIFTER.

ACTOR

- Remove an element v from A.

- For all $\alpha \in$ ACTION(STATE(v), a_{i+1}) do
  begin
    if α = 'accept' then r := TRUE;
    if α = 'shift' then add $\langle v, s \rangle$ to Q;
    if α = 'reducep' then
      for all vertices w such that there exists a directed
      walk of length $2|$RHS(p)$|$ from v to w
      /* For ε-rules this is a trivial walk, i.e. $w = v$ */
      do add $\langle w, p \rangle$ to R
  end.

COMPLETER
- Remove an element $\langle w, p \rangle$ from R.
- N := LHS(p); s := GOTO(STATE(w), N).
- If there exists $u \in U_i$ such that STATE(u) = s then
  begin
    if there does not exist a path of length 2 from u to w then
      begin
        create a vertex z labeled N in Γ;
        create two arcs in Γ from u to z and from z to w;
        for all $v \in (U_i - A)$ do
        /* In the case of non-ε-grammars this loop executes for $v = u$ only */
          for all q such that 'reduce q' $\in$ ACTION(STATE(v), a_{i+1}) do
            for all vertices t such that there exists a directed walk of
            length $2|$RHS(q)$|$ from v to t that goes through vertex z
            do add $\langle t, q \rangle$ to R
      end
  end
    else /* i.e., when there does not exist $u \in U_i$ such that STATE(u) = s */
      begin
        create in Γ two vertices u and z labeled s and N respectively;
        create two arcs in Γ from u to z and from z to w;
        add u to both A and U_i
      end.

SHIFTER
- U_{i+1} := $\emptyset$.
- Repeat
    remove an element $\langle v, s \rangle$ from Q;
    create a vertex x labeled a_{i+1} in Γ;
    create an arc from x to v;
    if there exists a vertex $u \in U_{i+1}$ such that STATE(u) = s then
      create an arc from u to x

    else
      begin
        create a vertex u labeled s and an arc from u to x in Γ;
        add u to U_{i+1}
      end.
    until $Q = \emptyset$.

As noted earlier, the above recognition algorithm can be changed into a parsing algorithm to produce the shared parse forest among the different parses. In the parsing algorithm the elements of R are triples $\langle w, p, L \rangle$ where L is a list of vertices that represent RHS symbols of p. When a node z with label $N = \mathrm{LHS}(p)$ is created the vertices in L are made its sons. In the case where there was a length 2 path (u, z, w) already from u to w, the nodes in L are attached to z as its alternate set of sons according to the node packing mechanism. One should note that this algorithm creates ε-deriving non-terminals that may be shared as a son by other non-terminals that are in ancestor-descendant relationship in the parse forest. To illustrate this point, the next section gives the complete parse graphs and corresponding parse trees for two example sentences. As an alternative, in building a parse forest one may replicate a null yielding subtree whenever this subtree participates in a reduction where at least one other sibling has non-empty yield. It is also plausible that one could precompile some subsets of each U_i that are obtained under the transitions with respect to null-deriving non-terminals.

5.5. Parsing Examples

Example 1: Consider the sentence xbbb $\in L(G_3)$. The complete parse graph for this sentence is shown in Figure 5.6. The dotted lines indicate the rejected paths. Table 5.1 is used to construct the graph. The parse tree for the same sentence is depicted in Figure 5.7. The shared non-terminal is shown in italics in both figures.

Example 2: Consider the sentence bbbx $\in L(G_3^r)$. A parse table for G_3^r can be given as Table 5.4. The figures 5.8 and 5.9 illustrate the parse graph and the parse tree of this sentence. One may observe that these are different from the parse graph and the parse tree that one can obtain by using Tomita's original algorithm for ε-grammars [9]. The modified recognizer creates a single A node in the parse graph whereas Tomita's recognizer will create three A vertices. In the new representation of the parse tree, the null yielding subtree with root A is shared among the S nodes that are descendants of each other. However as it was noted in Section 5.4, the parser could replicate such subtrees in the parse tree if one wishes so.

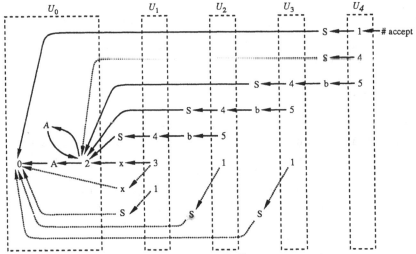

Figure 5.6. Parse graph for sentence xbbb $\in L(G_3)$.

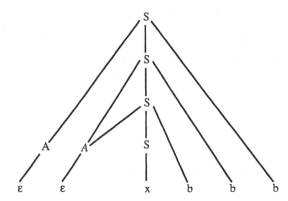

Figure 5.7. Parse tree for sentence xbbb $\in L(G_3)$.

5.6. Parsing Cyclic Grammars

Although the motivation for the current modification was to accommodate the non-cyclic ε-grammars within the GLR parsing method, but it turns out that the cyclic grammars with/without ε-rules can also be handled within this framework if one adopts an Earley's like convention [2] to represent the infinite parse trees. In this representation, the infinite number of parse trees may be encoded by introducing directed cycles in a parse tree. As an example, the parse "tree" for the sentence "x" $\in L(G_1)$ may be represented as Figure 5.10.

One may note that parsing of cyclic grammars does not need any additional mechanism apart from the packed shared forest as described in [9,10]. In fact,

Table 5.4. *Parse table for sentence bbbx* $\in L(G_3^r)$

State	x	b	#	A	S
0	sh3	sh2			1
1			acc		
2	sh3	sh2		4	
3			re2		
4			re3	5	
5			re1		
		Action table		*Goto table*	

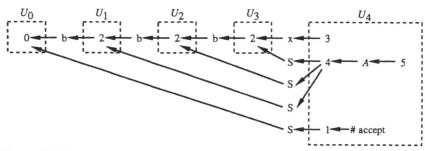

Figure 5.8. Parse graph of sentence in Table 5.4.

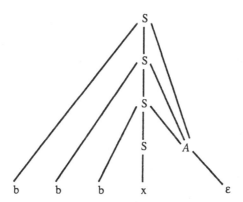

Figure 5.9. Parse tree of sentence in Table 5.4.

this approach can also be used with Tomita's original algorithm to parse the cyclic grammars which do not contain problem causing ε-rules. However as it was noted earlier, in the absence of a strong non-context-free evidence to select one interpretation of a "cyclic tree" (Figure 5.10) over its infinite number of interpretations, there seems to be little interest in employing of cyclic grammars for syntactic analysis.

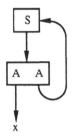

Figure 5.10. Parse tree for the sentence "x" $\in L(G_1)$.

5.7. Concluding Remarks

This chapter considered a modification on Tomita's parsing algorithm. Some ε-grammars, including cyclic grammars, that caused a problem in the original algorithm can now be handled within the framework of GLR parsing. The modified algorithm may introduce cycles in the parse graph in a restricted way in order to parse the null string between two adjacent input symbols . This makes the parse graph in the new algorithm a cyclic directed graph in some general cases. However, the new algorithm works exactly like the original one in case of grammars that have no ε-productions. This algorithm has no extra costs beyond that of the original algorithm.

Although no formal proof was provided here but it is believed that the modified algorithm is a precompiled equivalent of Earley's algorithm with respect to its coverage. The resulting algorithm suggests that the GLR parsers with graph structures and shared packed forests can be used for parsing the broader class of arbitrary context-free grammars.

Acknowledgements

The author would like to thank the program committee and the participants in the Carnegie Mellon Workshop on Parsing Technologies where this research was first presented. Special thanks goes to Masaru Tomita for organizing the workshop and putting this collection together.

The research reported here was supported by a grant from the Natural Sciences and Engineering Research Council of Canada.

References

[1] A.V. Aho and J.D. Ullman, The Theory of Parsing, Translation, and Compiling, Volume 1, Prentice Hall, Englewood Cliffs, NJ, 1972.
[2] J. Earley, An Efficient Context-free Parsing Algorithm, Ph.D. Thesis, Computer Science Department, Carnegie-Mellon University, Pittsburg, PA, 1968.
[3] J. Earley, An efficient context-free parsing algorithm, CACM, vol. 13, no. 2, February 1970, pp. 94-102.

[4] S.C. Johnson, YACC: Yet Another Compiler-Compiler, Technical Report 32, Bell Laboratories, Murray Hill, NJ, 1975. Also reproduced in Unix Programmer's Manual.

[5] M.P. Marcus, A Theory of Syntactic Recognition for Natural Language, MIT Press, Cambridge, MA, 1980.

[6] R. Nozohoor-Farshi, Handling of ill-designed grammars in Tomita's parsing algorithm, Proceedings of the International Workshop on Parsing Technologies, Carnegie Mellon University, Pittsburgh, PA, August 1989, pp. 182-192.

[7] R. Nozohoor-Farshi, On formalizations of Marcus' parser, COLING' 86, Proceedings of the 11th International Conference on Computational Linguistics, University of Bonn, West Germany, August 1986, pp. 533-535.

[8] R. Nozohoor-Farshi, LRRL(k) Grammars: A Left to Right Parsing Technique with Reduced Lookaheads, Ph.D. Thesis, Department of Computing Science, University of Alberta, Edmonton, Canada, 1986.

[9] M. Tomita, Efficient Parsing for Natural Language, Kluwer Academic Publishers, Boston, MA, 1986.

[10] M. Tomita, An efficient augmented-context-free parsing algorithm, Computational Linguistics, vol. 13, no. 1-2, January 1987, pp. 31-46.

6   Parallel GLR Parsing Based on Logic Programming

Hozumi Tanaka and Hiroaki Numazaki

To provide an efficient parser for natural language sentences, a parallel parsing algorithm is desirable. By realizing this fact, this paper presents an efficient parallel parser which analyzes syntactic ambiguities of a natural language sentence parallely.

The basic idea of our parallel parser is based on Tomita's parsing algorithm (Tomita, 1986) which adapted the LR parsing algorithm (Knuth, 1965) to context free grammars. The algorithm makes use of a breadth-first strategy to handle ambiguities of an input sentence. As the breadth first strategy is compatible with parallel processing, we can easily develop a parallel generalized LR parser with this strategy.

Our parallel parser named PGLR is implemented in GHC – a concurrent logic programming language developed by Japanese 5th generation computer project.

The implementation of PGLR is very efficient because all entries of the LR parsing table are translated into processes which conduct shift and reduce operations. Each process of PGLR has a Tree Structured Stack which is easily described as a list data structure of Logic Programming Languages.

6.1. Introduction

In order to get a high speed processing of natural language, a parallel processing technique is desirable. This paper presents an efficient parallel parser which analyzes in parallel syntactic ambiguities of the natural language sentences.

The basic idea of our parallel parser is based on Tomita's parsing algorithm (Tomita, 1986) which adapted the LR parsing algorithm to context free grammars. The algorithm makes use of a breadth-first strategy to handle ambiguities of an input sentence. As the breadth first strategy is compatible with parallel processing, we can easily develop a parallel generalized LR parser with this strategy. Our parallel parser named PGLR is implemented in GHC – a concurrent logic programming language developed by Japanese 5th generation computer project.

In order to avoid duplications of parsing, PGLR makes use of Tree Structured Stacks (TSS) in which top elements of the stacks having the same states are merged into one node, although Tomita's algorithm utilizes a Graph Structured

Stack (GSS). Why we do not use GSS is that an efficient implementation of GSS is rather difficult than that of TSS in the framework of Logic Programming.

One of the most siginificant feature of PGLR is to regard each entry of a LR parsing table as a process. The process has a stack and conducts a shift or a reduce operation of the stack. The conflicts in a LR table requires two or more operations, during which the process does all the operations required and at each time after a shift operation is carried out, a merge stack process is called to get Tree Structured Stack.

PGLR can handle a Definite Clause Grammar (Pereira, 1980), each rule of which has augmentations for testing applicability of the rule and gives information for parsing a sentence.

Before explaining how we can get PGLR from a LR parsing table, we will give a brief introduction of generalized LR parsing algorithm in Section 6.2 and the concurrent logic programming language GHC in Section 6.3. In Section 6.4 we describe an implementation of PGLR. In Section 6.5 we show how PGLR processes run in parallel. In Section 6.6 we discuss our future works of running PGLR on an actual parallel machine. In the last section, we give a conclusion of this paper.

6.2. A Generalized LR Parsing Algorithm

The LR parsing algorithm is one of the most efficient parsing algorithm because it runs deterministically for any LR grammar, a subset of context free grammars. Executions of the algorithm is guided by a LR parsing table which is obtained from a given LR grammar. Unfortunately, LR grammar is too weak to parse natural language sentences. When we apply this algorithm to a context free grammar, it is usual that conflicting entries which require two or more operations to the LR parser occur in a table. In order to get all parse trees of an input sentence, the LR parser have to try every operations in a conflicting entry encountered. There are two kinds of strategies to handle such conflicts:

- A Depth-First Strategy
- A Breadth-First Strategy

Nilsson (1986) has adopted a depth first strategy and Tomita (1986) a breadth first strategy. With these strategies, we can get all parse trees of a natural language sentence. We call those algorithms a generalized LR parsing algorithm.

Figure 6.1 shows an ambiguous English grammar and Figure 6.2 a LR parsing table generated from Figure 6.1. The LR parsing table consists of two parts: an action part (left-hand side) and a goto part (right-hand side).

Action part entries are specified by a parser's state (the row of the table) and a look-ahead preterminal(the column of the table) of an input sentence. There are two kinds of stack operations: shift and reduce operations. The symbol "sh N" in some entries indicates that the LR parser has to push a look-ahead preterminal

	(1)	S	$\rightarrow$	NP, VP
	(2)	S	$\rightarrow$	S, PP
	(3)	NP	$\rightarrow$	NP, RELC
	(4)	NP	$\rightarrow$	NP, PP
	(5)	NP	$\rightarrow$	det, noun
	(6)	NP	$\rightarrow$	noun
	(7)	NP	$\rightarrow$	pron
	(8)	VP	$\rightarrow$	v, NP
	(9)	RELC	$\rightarrow$	relp, VP
	(10)	PP	$\rightarrow$	p, NP

Figure 6.1. Ambiguous English grammar.

	det	noun	pron	v	p	relp	$	NP	PP	VP	RELC	S
0	sh1	sh2	sh3					5				4
1		sh6										
2				re6	re6	re6	re6					
3				re7	re7	re7	re7					
4					sh7		acc		8			
5				sh10	sh7	sh9			12	11	13	
6				re5	re5	re5	re5					
7	sh1	sh2	sh3					14				
8					re2		re2					
9				sh10						15		
10	sh1	sh2	sh3					16				
11					re1		re1					
12				re4	re4	re4	re4					
13				re3	re3	re3	re3					
14				re10	sh7/re10	sh9/re10	re10		12		13	
15				re9	re9	re9	re9					
16				re8	sh7/re8	sh9/re8	re8		12		13	

Figure 6.2. LR parsing table obtained from Figure 6.1 grammar.

on the stack and go to state N. The symbol "re N" means that the LR parser has to reduce from the top of the stack the number of elements equivalent to that of the right-hand side symbols of the rule numbered N. The symbol "acc" means that the LR parser has successfully completed parsing. If an entry contains no operation, the LR parser detect an error.

The right-hand side table entry indicates which state the LR parser should enter after a reduce operation. The LR table shown in Figure 6.2 has 2 conflicts at state 11 (row number 11) and state 12 for the column "p." Each of the conflicting two entries contains a shift and a reduce operations and is called a shift-reduce conflict. When the generalized LR parser encounters a conflict, it tries all operations to get all parse trees. In those case, PGLR parser generates concurrent processes each of which tries one operation in the entry.

```
(1)  a:- true |
         b(Stream),
         c(Stream).
(2)  b(Stream):- true |
         Stream=[ x|Rest ],
         b(Rest).
(3)  c([ A|Stream1 ]):- true |
         c(Stream1).
```

Figure 6.3. Typical Statement of GHC.

6.3. Brief Introduction to GHC

Before explaining the details of PGLR, we will give a brief introduction to GHC, typical statements of which are given in Figure 6.3. The vertical bar in a GHC statement (Figure 6.3) functions like a cut symbol of Prolog. When a goal "a" is called, the process of statement (1) is activated and subgoals "b (Stream)" and "c (Stream)" are executed simultaneously. In GHC, this is called AND-parallel execution. In other words, subprocesses "b (Stream)" and "c (Stream)" are created by a parent process "a" and they run in parallel. Note that the definition of process "c" in statement (3) is going to instantiate the variable "Stream" in "c (Stream)" with "[A | Stream1]." In such a case the execution of process "c" will be suspended until "Stream" has been instantiated by process "b (Stream)." By the recursive process call in the body of definition (2), process "b" continues to produce the atom "x" and places it on stream. The atom "x" is sent to process "c" by the GHC stream communication; process "c" continues to consume atom "x" on stream.

6.4. Implementation of PGLR

PGLR is implemented in GHC which is a concurrent logic programming language developed by Japanese 5th generation computer project. In our system, each entry in a LR parsing table is regarded as a process which will handle shift and reduce operations. If the process discovers a conflict in a LR parsing table, the process copies its own stack and sends it to subprocesses which conduct reduce operations. After finishing the reduce operations, a merge process will be activated if necessary.

To avoid recomputations of parsing, Tomita has devised a Graph Structured Stack (GSS) in which stack top elements with the same states will be merged. However, GSS is not so a simple data structure that the simplest way to implement GSS is to use side effects. But side effects are not desirable for us to simulate GSS, because we are going to implement GSS in the framework of a logic programming language, GHC.[1]

---

1. In the paper (Tanaka, 1989), we have shown a generalized LR parser without using GSS.

In our implementation of PGLR, in order to simulate GSS, we use a Tree Structured Stack(TSS). Consider the following two stacks:

$$(top) \ [7, P, 4, S, 0] \ (bottom)$$

$$(top) \ [7, P, 16, NP, 10, V, 5, NP, 0] \ (bottom)$$

The top element of two stacks being the same, "7,P," we can be able to merge these top two elements and will get the following TSS:

$$[7, P, [4, S, 0], [16, NP, 10, V, 5, NP, 0]]$$

6.4.1. Description of PGLR Algorithm

Consider that an input sentence is consisted of a sequence of preterminals, "p1 p2 ... pn." PGLR begins activating a sequence of action processes, "p1,p2,...,pn,p$" for each preterminals of an input sentence. Here, the process "p$" corresponds to the end of the input sentence. At first, only one action process "p1" becomes active, and all the other processes are suspended until stack information is sent by an active process. The action process "p1" is initially given a stack with state "0." It carries out a shift operation specified by a LR table, sends the new stack information to "p2," and then terminates. The activated action process "pi" performs shift or reduce operations and sends new stack information to the process "pi+1" which is will be currently activated. If the rightmost action process "p$" is activated and finds out an "acc" entry in the LR table, PGLR ends with success. If we have a conflict during parsing, more than two subprocesses will be activated simultaneously and run in parallel. There are four kinds of processes which are activated during parsing.

1. *Action process*: Action processes perform the operations specified by an entry of the "action table." The details of action processes will be explained later with sample definitions.

2. *Reduce process*: A reduce process pops the appropriate portion of the stack and creates a partially parsed tree by applying a grammar rule specified in the reduce entry. And then the reduce process activates a goto process to shift the state into a new one. Suppose, in the course of a reduce operation, the reduce process finds out many branches on a stack, the reduce operation for every branch should be carried out. In order to do so, the reduce process creates a subprocess for the reduce operation.

3. *Goto process*: A goto process performs a shift operation specified in the entry of the "goto table." The goto process is activated after the reduce operation.

4. *Merge_stack process*: A merge_stack process receives a number of stacks from both action processes and goto processes. In case of having many stacks whose top elements are same, the merge_stack process merges them into a tree structured stack. The definition of "merge_stack" is shown in Appendix 6.A.

6.4.2. Definition of Action Process

Followings are examples of definitions of action processes which carry out a shift, a reduce, an accept, and an error operation.

Activating action processes.   In order to parse a sentence, PGLR begins activating AND-parallel action processes which corresponds to a sequence of preterminals in an input sentence. If the input sentence is "Doors open," the initial goal becomes as following:

```
?- noun_0([[0]], [noun,doors], Stacks1),
     v_0(Stacks1,[v,open], Stacks2),
     $_0(Stacks2,[ ],Result).
```

The first argument of an action process is a set of stacks sent by the preceding action processes. The second argument is a pair of a preterminal and a word which will be an element pushed on the stack by shift operations. The third argument is a new stack calculated by this action process. The following is a definition of the first process "noun_0" in the initial goal.

```
noun_0([ ], __, Out):- true |
     Out = [ ].
noun_0([[No | Stack] | Rest], T, Out):- true |
     noun(No, [No | Stack], T, Stacks1),
     noun_0(Rest, T, Stacks2),
     merge_stacks(Stacks1, Stacks2, Out).
```

In the body of the second clause, the processes "noun," "noun_0," and "merge_stacks" are activated in parallel. Depending on the value of "No," the process "noun" performs a shift or reduce operation. The reason why the process "noun_0" is called recursively is that every stack in the first argument should be examined. The process "merge_stacks" merges all stacks calculated by the process "noun" and "noun_0."

Shift operation.   An action process creates a pair of a look-ahead preterminal and a new state specified by a shift entry, pushes it on a stack, and finally terminates by itself. The description of the "sh 2" entry of the column "noun" and the row "0" in Figure 6.2 for example is as follows:

```
noun(0, Stack, T, NStacks) :- true |
     NStacks=[[2,T| Stack]].
```

In the above process definition, the first argument of "noun" is a state of the top element of "Stack." The third argument "T" is a leaf of parsing tree, namely a pair of a preterminal and a terminal symbol of the input sentence. The fourth argument "NStacks" is a set of stacks calculated by this action process. In the body of this definition, a pair of state 2 and "T" is pushed onto "Stack."

Reduce operation. An action process activates a reduce process which is given a copy of stack information by the action process. The reduce process returns a reduced stack to the action process. After getting a reduced stack, the action process activates the same action process recursively which looks for another actions. Consider the entry of state "2" and a look-ahead preterminal "v" in Figure 6.2. The definition of an action process "v" is:

```
v(2, [_,T1| Stack], T, NStacks) :- true |
    reduce(1, 6, Stack, [T1], NStacks1),
    v_0(NStacks1, T, NStacks).
```

In the body of an action process "v," two processes, "reduce" and "v_0" are activated simultaneously. The process "reduce" conducts a reduce and goto operation by which the action process moves to a new state. The reason why the action process "v_0" is activated recursively is that the look-ahead preterminal remains the same (namely "v") after a reduce process runs.

Shift/reduce operation. At first, a shift operation and reduce operations are carried out, and then the action process activates a merge process which will merge two stacks, each of which is obtained by the shift and reduce operations.

Consider an entry of state "14" and a look-ahead preterminal "p" in Figure 6.2. We will find out a shift-reduce conflict, "sh 7/re 10." The definition of an action process "p" is:

```
p(14, [14, T1mid Stack], T, NStacks) :- true |
    reduce(1, 10, Stack, [T1], Stacks1),
    p_0(Stacks1, T, Stacks2),
    merge_stack([7,T,14,T1midStack], Stacks2, NStacks).
```

In the body of the process "p," subprocesses "reduce," "p_0," and "merge_stack" are activated simultaneously.

Reduce/reduce operation. An action process activates reduce processes and sends the stack information, each of which is a copy of the stack kept by the action process. After finishing reduce processes, the action process will activate a merge process to merge several stacks sent by reduce processes. Finally, in order to look for another actions, the action process activates the same action process recursively.

Accept operation. After an action process gets a result of parsing, it ends with success.

Consider an entry of state "4" and a look-ahead preterminal "$" in Figure 6.2, we will find out "acc" which indicates a success of parsing. The definition of the action process "$" is:

```
$(4, [_, Tree|_], _, Result) :- true |
    Result=Tree.
```

"Tree" becomes the final output ("Result") of parsing.

Error operation.   If no operation is specified in an entry, an error handling process will be activated. We have to define an error handling process in some states if necessary. The following is a definition of an error process for a look-ahead preterminal "noun." The following definition has to be placed at the end of "noun" processes:

```
otherwise.
det(S, Stack, __, NStacks) :- true |
    NStacks=[ ].
```

In the GHC statements given below "otherwise" will be executed if all GHC statements above "otherwise" fails.

6.4.3. Definition of Reduce Process

The definition of a reduce process is as follows:

```
reduce(0, N, Stacks, T, NStacks):- true|
    re(N, Stacks, T, NStacks).
reduce(M, N,[S,T1|Stack],T, NStacks, Tail):- integer(S)|
    M1 := M-1,
    reduce(M1, N, St1, [T1|T], NStacks).
otherwise.
reduce(_, _, [ ], _, NStacks):- true|
    NStacks = [ ].
reduce(M, N, [[_,T1|Stack]|Rest], T, NStacks):- true|
    M1 := M-1,
    reduce(M1, N, Stack, [T1|T], NStacks1),
    reduce(M, N, Rest, T, NStacks2),
    merge(NStacks1, NStacks2, NStacks).
```

In the body of the first reduce process, a subprocess "re" is activated. In the body of the second reduce process, a subprocess "reduce" is activated recursively to get the reduced stack. The fourth reduce process deals with a Tree Structured Stack which has many branches. In the body of the process, every branch is brought one by one and is sent to a subprocess "reduce." The first argument of reduce processes is the number of elements to be reduced. The second argument is a rule number which is used for the reduce operation.

After finishing all reduce operations, a process "re" is activated to create a partially parsed tree using a rule for the reduce operation. Following is a sample definition of the process "re."

```
re(1,[S |Stack],T,NStacks):- true |
    s(S,[S |Stack],[sentence |T],NStacks).
re(2,[S |Stack],T,S,NStack):- true |
    s(S,[S |Stack],[sentence |T],NStacks).
re(3,[S |Stack],T,NStacks):- true |
    np(S,[S |Stack],[np |T],NStacks).
```

re(4,[S |Stack],T,NStacks):- true |
   . . .

The number in the first argument is a rule number that is used by the reduce operation. In the body, a goto process is activated to shift a new state.

6.4.4. Definition of Goto Process

After a reduce operation is finished, a goto process is activated to push a new element on the stack. The element is a pair of partially parsed tree and a new state specified by the goto table. Definition of a sample of goto process is given below:

```
np(0,Stack,T,NStacks):- true|
    NStacks = [[5,T|Stack]].
np(7,Stack,T,NStacks):- true|
    NStacks = [[14,T|Stack]].
np(10,Stack,T,NStacks):- true|
    NStacks = [[16,T|Stack]].
otherwise.
np(_, [ ], _,NStacks):- true |
    NStacks = [ ].
np(_, [[S|Stack] | Rest], T, NStacks):- true |
    np(S, [S|Stack],T,Stacks1),
    np([ ], Rest, T, Stacks2),
    merge_stack(Stacks1, Stacks2, NStacks).
```

6.4.5. An Example of PGLR Parsing

Following is a trace of parsing by PGLR parser:

input sentence : i open the door with a key .

Parsing begins with activating AND-parallel action processes each of which corresponds to a preterminal of the input sentence. However, only the first action process "pron_0" will be executed and the other processes will be suspended until "Stack1," "Stack2," . . ., "Stack8" are instantiated one by one.

```
?- pron_0([[0]],[pron,i],Stack1),
   v_0(Stack1,[v,open],Stack2),
   det_0(Stack2,[det,the],Stack3),
   noun_0(Stack3,[noun,door],Stack4),
   p_0(Stack4,[p,with],Stack5),
   det_0(Stack5,[det,a],Stack6),
   noun_0(Stack7,[noun,key],Stack8),
   $_0(Stack8,[],Result).
```

Following is the actual output of tracing:

```
CALL   pron_0([[0]],[pron,i],Stack1)
CALL     pron(0,[0],[pron,i],Stack11)
```

```
EXIT      pron(0,[0],[pron,i],[[3,[pron,i],0]])
CALL      pron_0([],[pron,i],Stack12)
EXIT      pron_0([],[pron,i],[])
CALL      merge_stacks([[3,[pron,i],0]],[],Stack1)
EXIT      merge_stacks([[3,[pron,i],0]],[],[[3,[pron,i],0]])
EXIT    pron_0([[0]],[pron,i],[[3,[pron,i],0]])
CALL    v_0([[3,[pron,i],0]],[v,open],Stack2)
CALL      v([3,[[pron,i],0],[v,open],Stack21)
CALL        reduce(0,7,[0],[[pron,i]],Stack22)
CALL          re(7,[0],[[pron,i]],Stack22)
CALL            np(0,[0],[np,[pron,i]],Stack22)
EXIT            np(0,[0],[np,[pron,i]],[[5,[np,[pron,i]],0]])
EXIT          re(7,[0],[[pron,i]],[[5,[np,[pron,i]],0]])
EXIT        reduce(0,7,[0],[[pron,i]],[[5,[np,[pron,i]],0]])
CALL        v_0([[5,[np,[pron,i]],0]],[v,open],Stack21) : skip
EXIT        v_0([[5,[np,[pron,i]],0]],[...],[[10,[v,open],5,[np,...],0]])
            ...........................
EXIT    v_0([[3,[pron,i],0]],[...],[[10,[v,open],5...]])
CALL    det_0([[10,[v,open],5...]],[det,the],Stack3) : skip
EXIT    det_0([[10,[v,open],5...]],[det,the],[[1,[det,the],10,[v,open]...]])
CALL    noun_0([[1,[det,the],10,[v,open]...]],[noun,door],Stack4) : skip
EXIT    noun_0([[1,[det,the]...]],[...],[[6,[noun,door],1,[det,the]...]])
CALL    p_0([[6,[noun,door],1...]],[p,with],Stack5)
CALL      p(6,[6,[noun,door],1...]],[p,with],Stack51)
CALL        reduce(1,8,[1,[det,the],10...],[[noun,door]],Stack52) : skip
EXIT        reduce(1,8,[1...],[...],[[16,[np,[det,the],[noun,door]],10...]])
CALL      p_0([[16,[np...],10,[v...]...]],[p,with],Stack51)
CALL        p(16,[16,[np...],10,[v...]...],[p,with],Stack52)
CALL          reduce(1,8,[10,[v...]...],[[np,[det...],[noun...]],Stack53)
: skip
EXIT          reduce(1,8,[10...],[...],[[11,[vp,[v,open],[np...]],5...]])
CALL          p_0([[11,[vp...],5,[np...],0]],[p,with],Stack54)
CALL            p(11,[11,[vp...],5,[np...],0],[p,with],Stack55)
CALL              reduce(1,1,[5,[np...],0],[[vp,[v...],[np...]]],Stack56)
: skip
EXIT              reduce(1,1,[5...],[...],[[4,[sentence,[np...],[vp...]],0
CALL              p_0([[4,[sentence,[np...],[vp...]],0]],[p,with],Stack55)
CALL                p(4,[4,[sentence,[np...],[vp...]],0],[p,with],Stack57)
EXIT                p(4,[4...],[...],[[7,[p,with],4,[sentence...],0]])
            ...........................
EXIT              p_0([[4...]],[...],[[7,[p,with],4,[sentence...],0]])
EXIT            p(11,[11...0],[...],[[7,[p,with],4,[sentence...],0]])
```

```
                        . . . . . . . . . . . . . . . . . . . . . . . . . . . . .
EXIT        p_0([[11...]],[...],[[7,[p,with],4,[sentence...],0]])
CALL        merge_stack([7,[p,with],16,[np...]...],
                        [[7,[p,with],4,[sentence...],0]],Stack52)
EXIT        merge_stack([7,[p,with],16...],[[7,[p,with],4...]],
                        [[7,[p,with],[16...],[4...]]])
EXIT        p(16,[16...],[...],[[7,[p,with],[16...],[4...]]])
                        . . . . . . . . . . . . . . . . . . . . . . . . . . . . .
EXIT        p_0([[16...]],[...],[[7,[p,with],[16...],[4...]]])
EXIT        p(6,[6,[noun,door],1...],[...],[[7,[p,with],[16...],[4...]]])
                        . . . . . . . . . . . . . . . . . . . . . . . . . . . . .
EXIT    p_0([[6,[noun,door],1...],[...],[[7,[p,with],[16...],[4...]]])
                        . . . . . . . . . . . . . . . . . . . . . . . . . . . . .
CALL    $_0([[6,[noun,key],1,[det,a],7,[p...],[16...],[4...]]],[],Stack8)
CALL      $(6,[6,[noun,key],1...],[],Stack81)
CALL        reduce(1,5,[1,[det,a],7...],[[noun,door]],Stack82)
                        . . . . . . . . . . . . . . . . . . . . . . . . . . . . .
EXIT        reduce(1,5,[1...],[...],[[14,[np,[det,a],[...]],7,[p,with]...]])
CALL        $_0([[14,[np,[det,a],[...]],7,[p,with]...]],[],Stack81)
CALL          $(14,[14,[np...],7,[p,with],[16...],[4...]],[],Stack83)
CALL            reduce(1,10,[7,[p,with],[16...],[4...]],[[np...]],Stack84)
CALL              reduce(0,10,[[16...],[4...]],[[p,with],[np...]],Stack84)
CALL                re(10,[[16...],[4...]],[[p,with],[np...]],Stack84)
CALL                  pp([16...],[[16...],[4...]],[pp,[p...],[np...]],Stack84)
CALL                    pp(16,[16...],[pp...],Stack85)
EXIT                    pp(16,[16...],[pp...],[[12,[pp...],16...]])
CALL                    pp([],[[4...]],[pp...],Stack86)
CALL                      pp(4,[4...],[pp...],Stack87)
EXIT                      pp(4,[4...],[pp...],[[8,[pp...],4...]])
                        . . . . . . . . . . . . . . . . . . . . . . . . . . . . .
EXIT                  pp([...],[[16...],[4...]],[...],[[12...],[8...]])
                        . . . . . . . . . . . . . . . . . . . . . . . . . . . . .
EXIT        reduce(1,10,[7...],[...],[[12...],[8...]])
CALL        $_0([[12...],[8...]],[],Stack83)
CALL          $(12,[12,[pp...],16...],[],Stack88) : skip
EXIT          $(12,[12...],[...],
                    [[sentence,[np...],[vp,[v...],[np,[np...],[pp...]]]]])
CALL          $(8,[8,[pp...],4...],[],Stack89) : skip
EXIT          $(8,[8,[pp...],4...],[],
                    [[sentence,[sentence,[np...]],[vp...]],[pp...]]])
```

Sentence No.	Time (ms)	Number of Tree
1	280	2
2	180	1
3	680	15
4	940	14
5	2600	30
6	4420	56
7	27340	192
8	40760	200
9	5600	186

Figure 6.4. Elapsed time of parsing.

6.5. The Results of an Experiment

We used a Sun-3/260 workstation and GHC. The CFG grammar rules are shown in Appendix 6.B. Sample sentences to be parsed are:

1. I open the window.
2. Diagram is an augmented grammar.
3. The structural relations are holding among constituents.
4. It is not tied to a particular domain of applications.
5. Diagram analyzes all of the basic kinds of phrases and sentences.
6. This paper presents an explanatory overview of a large and complex grammar that is used in a sentence.
7. The annotations provide important information for other parts of the system that interpret the expression in the context of a dialogue.
8. For every expression it analyzes, diagram provides an annotated description of the structural relations holding among its constituents.
9. Procedures can also assign scores to an analysis, rating some applications of a rule as probable or as unlikely.

The elapsed time of parsing is shown in Figure 6.4.

6.6. Conclusion

It is a straightforward task for us to implement PGLR parser in GHC. The reason is that GHC has a very good mechanism for synchronization of processes. The significant feature of PGLR is that each entry of LR table is regarded as a process which handles shift and reduce operations. When a conflict occurs in an entry of LR table, the corresponding parsing process activates two or more subprocesses which run in parallel and simulate breadth first strategy. Each subprocess is given a stack information by the parent process.

The experiment has revealed that PGLR runs so fast that it will be a promising parser for processing many complex natural language sentences.

However, PGLR has many problems to be solved. For example, (1) How to handle gaps and idioms? (2) How to integrate syntactic and semantic processing? (3) Is there a good algorithm to distribute many processes among limited number of processors?

As the PGLR explained in this paper strictly scans input words from left to right, the number of processes which run in parallel will be limited in nature. It is valuable for us to look for better algorithm which enables us to extract more parallelism.

Appendix 6.A: Definition of merge_stack Process

```
merge_stacks([ ],Stacks,NStacks):- true |
    NStacks = Stacks.
merge_stacks(Stacks,[ ],NStacks):- true |
    NStacks = Stacks.
merge_stacks([Stack|Rest],Stacks,NStacks):- true |
    merge_stack(Stack,Stacks,NStacks1),
    merge_stacks(Rest,NStacks1,NStacks).
merge_stack(Stack,[ ],NStacks):- true |
    NStacks = [Stack].
merge_stack([S,T,S1|Stack1],[[S,T,S2|Stack2]|Rest],NStacks):-
integer(S1) |
    merge_stack1([S1|Stack1],[S2|Stack2],Stack3),
    NStacks = [[S,T|Stack3]|Rest].
otherwise.
merge_stack([S,T,S1|Stack1],[[S,T,S2|Stack2]|Rest],NStacks):-
true |
    merge_stack2([S1|Stack1],[S2|Stack2],Stack3),
    NStacks = [[S,T|Stack3]|Rest].
merge_stack(Stack,[Stack1|Rest],NStacks):- true |
    merge_stack(Stack,Rest,NStacks1),
    NStack = [Stack1 | NStacks1].
merge_stack1(Stack1,[S2|Stack2],Stack3):- integer(S2) |
    Stack3=[Stack1,[S2|Stack2]].
otherwise.
merge_stack1(Stack1,Stack2,Stack3):- true |
    Stack3=[Stack1|Stack2].
merge_stack2(Stack1,[S2|Stack2],Stack3):- integer(S2) |
    Stack3=[[S2|Stack2]|Stack1].
otherwise.
merge_stack2(Stack1,Stack2,Stack3):- true |
    merge(Stack1, Stack2, Stack3).
```

Appendix 6.B: Grammar Rules

advp → adv.	advp → as,advp,ascomp.	advp → as,advp.
advp → p,sdec.	ncomp → pp.	ncomp → of,np.
ncomp → vp2.	ncomp → srel.	ncomp → adjp.
ncomp → ncomp,pp.	ncomp → infinitrel.	modalp → modal.
modalp → modal,nt.	vp3 → vp.	vp3 → pred.
vp3 → nt,vp3.	infinitrel → vp.	infinitrel → be,vp.
vp2 → v.	vp2 → v,advp.	vp2 → v,adjp.
vp2 → vp2,advp.	vp2 → vp2,pp.	gerund → vp.

gerund → nt,vp.
pp → p,np,paraconj,np.
aux → bep.
adjp → adj.
adjp → adjp,paraconj,adjp.
pred → np.
pred → pred,pp.
nomhd → v,nomhd.
ddet → nt,all.
ddet → nt,all,det.
vp → v,p,advp.
vp → v,adjp.
vp → v,sdec.
vp → v,obj,adjp.
vp → v,obj,advp.
vp → vp,advp.
sdec → subj,adv,vp.
sdec → subj,adv,auxd,vp.
sdec → subj,bep,adv,pred.
sdec → subj,aux,bep,pred.
sdec → subj,aux,adv,bep,adv,pred.
sdec → subj,adv,be.
sdec → sdec,comma,vp3.
np → nomhd.
np → a,nomhd,ncomp.
np → a,ncomp.
np → pron.
np → ddet,adjp,nomhd,ncomp.
np → gerund.
np → relpro,sdec.
sentence → sdec.
sentence → pp,comma,sentence.
srel → relpro,bep,pred.

pp → p,obj.
bep → be.
aux → modalp.
adjp → ddet,adj.
adjp → adv,adjp.
pred → pp.
nomhd → n.
ddet → det.
ddet → all,det.
obj → np.
vp → v,advp.
vp → v,vp.
vp → v,np,relpro,sdec.
vp → v,obj,vp.
vp → v,obj,be,pred.
vp → vp,paraconj,adjp.
sdec → subj,auxd,vp.
sdec → subj,adv,auxd,adv,vp.
sdec → subj,adv,bep,pred.
sdec → subj,aux,bep,adv,pred.
sdec → subj,adv,aux,be.
sdec → subj,be.
sdec → sdec,advp.
np → nomhd,ncomp.
np → ddet,nomhd.
np → ddet.
np → pron,ncomp.
np → ddet,adjp,ncomp.
np → as,adj,of,np.
np → np,paraconj,np.
sentence → sdec,paraconj,sdec.
sentence → advp,comma,sentence.
srel → subj,vp2.

pp → p,np,of,np.
bep → be,nt.
auxd → aux.
adjp → as,adjp.
pred → adjp.
pred → vp2.
nomhd → adjp,nomhd.
ddet → all.
ddet → all,of,det.
vp → v.
vp → v,np.
vp → v,obj.
vp → v,relpro,sdec.
vp → v,advp,obj.
vp → vp,pp.
sdec → subj,vp.
sdec → subj,auxd,adv,vp.
sdec → subj,bep,pred.
sdec → subj,adv,bep,adv,pred.
sdec → subj,aux,adv,bep,pred.
sdec → subj,aux,be.
sdec → vp3,comma,sdec.
sdec → sdec,comma,advp.
np → a,nomhd.
np → ddet,nomhd,ncomp.
np → ddet,ncomp.
np → ddet,adjp,nomhd.
np → det,gerund.
np → as,adj,np.
np → np,comma,np.
sentence → sdec,comma,paraconj,sdec
srel → relpro,vp.
subj → np.

References

Aho, A. V. and Ulman, J. D. (1972). *The Theory of Parsing, Translation, and Compiling*, Prentice-Hall, Englewood Cliffs, New Jersey.

Aho, A. V., Senthi, R., and Ulman, J. D. (1985). *Compilers Principles, Techniques, and Tools*, Addison-Wesley.

Fuch, K., Furukawa, K., and Mizoguchi, F. (1987). *Heiretu Ronri Gata Gengo GHC To Sono Ouyou*, Kyoritsu Syuppan (Japanese).

Knuth, D. E. *On the translation of languages from left to right*, Information and Control 8:6, pp. 607–639.

Konno, A. and Tanaka, H. (1986). *Hidari Gaichi Wo Kouryo Shita Bottom Up Koubun Kaiseki*, Computer Softwear, Vol. 3, No. 2, pp. 115–125 (Japanese).

Nakata, I. (1981). *Compiler*, Sangyo Tosyo (Japanese).

Matsumoto, Y. and Sugimura, R. (1986). *Ronri Gata Gengo Ni Motodsuku Koubun Kaiseki System SAX*, Computer Softwear, Vol. 3, No. 4, pp. 4–11 (Japanese).

Matsumoto, Y. (1987). *A Parallel Parsing System for Natural Language Analysis*, New Generation Computing, Vol. 5, No. 1, pp. 63–78.

Matsumoto, Y. (June 1989). *Natural Language Parsing Systems based on Logic Programming*,

Ph.D thesis of Kyoto University.

Mellish, C. S. (1985). *Computer Interpretation of Natural Language Descriptions*, Ellis Horwood Limited.

Nilsson, U. (1986). *AID: An Alternative Implementation of DCGs*, New Generation Computing, 4, pp. 383–399.

Tanaka, H. and Numazaki, H. (1989). *Parallel Generalized LR Parsing based on Logic Programming*, International Workshop on Parsing Technologies, pp. 329–338.

Okumura, M. (1989). *Sizengengo Kaiseki Ni Okeru Imiteki Aimaisei Wo Zoushinteki Ni Kaisyou Suru Keisan Model*, Natural Language Analysis Working Group, Information Processing Society of Japan, NL71-1 (Japanese).

Pereira, F. and Warren, D. (1980). Definite Clause Grammar for Language Analysis - A Survey of the Formalism and a Comparison with Augmented Transition Networks, *Artif. Intell*, Vol. 13, No. 3, pp .231–278.

Tokunaga, T., Iwayama, M., Kamiwaki, T., and Tanaka, H. (1988). *Natural Language Analysis System LangLAB*, Transactions of Information Processing Society of Japan, Vol. 29, No. 7, pp. 703–711 (Japanese).

Tomita, M. (1986). *Efficient Parsing for Natural Language*, Kluwer Academic Publishers.

Tomita, M. (1987). *An Efficien Augmented-Context-Free Parsing Algorithm*, Computational Linguistics, Vol. 13, Numbers 1–2, pp. 31–46.

Ueda, K. (1985). *Guarded Horn Clauses*, Proc. The Logic Programming Conference, Lecture Notes in Computer Science, 221.

Uehara, K. and Toyoda, J. (1983). *Sakiyomi To Yosokukinou Wo Motsu Jutugo Ronri Gata Koubun Kaiseki Program : PAMPS*, Transactions of Information Processing Society of Japan, Vol. 24, No. 4, pp. 496–504 (Japanese).

7   GLR Parsing with Scoring

Keh-Yih Su, Jong-Nae Wang, Mei-Hui Su, and Jing-Shin Chang

7.1. Introduction

In a machine translation system, the number of possible analyses associated
with a given sentence is usually very large due to the ambiguous nature of
natural languages. But, it is desirable that only the *best* one or two analyses
be translated and passed to the post-editor so as to reduce the required efforts
of post-editing. In addition, processing time for a sentence is usually limited
when processing a large number of sentences in batch mode. Therefore, it is
important, in a practical machine translation system, to obtain the *best* syntax
tree which has the *best* annotated semantic interpretation within a *reasonably
short time*. This is only possible with an intelligent parsing algorithm which
can truncate undesirable analyses as early as possible and avoid wasting time
in parsing those ambiguous constructions that will eventually be discarded.

Since the selected analysis has to be the *best* in a meaningful sense (for
example, best in probabilistic sense), it means that a good *scoring mechanism*
will play a very important role. A *score function* which has such optimality
property will be described in this chapter.

There are several methods to accelerate the parsing process [Su 88b], one of
which is to decrease the size of the *searching space* in the whole parsing state
space. This can be accomplished with a *scored* parsing algorithm that truncates
unlikely paths as early as possible [Su 87b] and hence decreases the parsing
time. Such parsing strategy is referred to as scored truncation.

The searching strategy for a scored parsing algorithm can be either parallel or
sequential. A *parallel truncation* algorithm ([Su 87b]) would expand the parsing
state space in the breadth-first direction, which allows a number of, say N,
alternative paths to expand at the end of each step. A typical parallel truncation
algorithm is the beam search algorithm in AI literatures. A *sequential truncation*
algorithm, on the other hand, would branch in the depth-first direction. This
strategy has some advantages over its parallel counterpart. First, it is faster
in getting the *first* parse than the parallel approach. This feature makes it
possible to get a fast response if the system is facilitated with a good scoring
mechanism, and it can be beneficial for systems which select the first parse
as their goal. (This is often the case for small MT systems.) Once the first
parse is acquired, we can also use its score to establish a lower bound for all
possible scores; any parse whose score is lower than this lower bound can be

safely truncated. Thus, we can use this bound to speed up the parsing process further. Secondly, it is much easier to implement a sequential truncation version than a parallel one, and it takes less memory space in the sequential version because no multiple temporary copies of different analyses need to be saved. Finally, the sequential truncation strategy can cut down more searching space than its parallel counterpart because it will try less paths when a good scoring mechanism is given.

Furthermore, a real system usually set a time limit to stop the parsing process when a sentence is taking too long to parse because of its long sentence length or complicated structure. Under such circumstances, the sequential searching strategy is better than the parallel approach because we are likely to have some complete syntax trees to work with even if the parsing was suspended abnormally when its time expires. On the other hand, the parallel approach will not have this advantage because it may not have any on-going path that traverse to the end.

In this chapter, we will give an informal introduction to the *Score Function* used in our machine translation system. Some desirable features of this score function will be described and its application to Generalized LR parsing is introduced. We will also propose a *sequential truncation* parsing algorithm to reduce the searching space of the parsing process, and hence improving the parsing efficiency. This algorithm employs the score function proposed in [Su 88a], which takes advantages of the probabilistic characteristics of the syntactic and semantic information in the sentences. Preliminary tests on this algorithm were conducted with some special versions of our machine translation system, the ARCHTRAN [Su 87a], and encouraging results were observed. Readers interested in the parallel version of the scored truncation parsing mechanism can refer to [Su 87b] for more details.

7.2. Making Decisions With The Score Function

7.2.1. Definition of the Score Function

In a scored parsing system, the best analysis is selected base on its score. Several scoring mechanisms have been proposed in the literatures [Robi 83, Benn 85, Gars 87, Su 88a]. The one we adopt is the *score function* proposed in [Su 88a]. This score function measures the degree of preference of a semantically annotated syntax tree by the following general formula:

$$SCORE(Sem, Syn, Lex, Words) \equiv P(Sem, Syn, Lex | Words)$$

where *Sem*, *Syn* and *Lex* are the particular *semantic interpretation*, *syntactic structure* and *lexical feature* attached to a given ambiguous construction whose terminal strings are *Words*. In other words, we will assign a higher score to a semantically annotated construction if it is often regarded as the *most probable* interpretation to the terminal strings. The score function defined in this way is not only linguistically significant but also statistically optimal as we shall show later. Hence, it provides a way to bridge the gap between linguistic knowledge and statistic reality.

7.2.2. Why Score Function

The above probabilistic model has some advantages over traditional rule-based approaches, which are usually *ad hoc*. First of all, because the score function is statistics-based, it is more objective (in statistic sense) than the certainty factors assigned by linguistic experts (linguists) in a rule-based expert system; a score of 0.8 defined in *statistic sense* will be significantly different from a certainty factor of 0.8 assigned in *expert's sense*. It is also much easier to *train* and *maintain* the probability entries than linguistic rules. Furthermore, the embedded knowledge in the statistic database is always *consistent* in statistic sense, as opposed to conventional knowledge bases, which usually contain some degree of inconsistency. Another advantage of this score function lies in its flexible *extensibility*. It can be extended easily to lower linguistic levels such as acoustics, phonetics and morphology. On the other hand, it can also be extended to a higher level such as pragmatics. In fact, we have already extended its definition to deal with speech recognition in some applications [Chia 89].

The most striking feature of the above score function is its *optimality* when used as the preference measure of semantically annotated syntax trees. (We will take a syntax tree annotated with semantic features as the representation of a specific interpretation to a given sentence throughout our discussion.) To see why it is *optimal* as the preference measure, let's consider the following situation. In an attempt to find the best annotated syntax tree among the ambiguous ones, we must pay some price for possible *misjudgement* no matter what scoring mechanism is used. In general, we want the cost to be minimal. The problem of finding an optimal scoring function can thus be formulated as a *cost minimization* problem. Suppose that we will incur a loss (or cost) of C_1 when we make a right choice on the semantic interpretation (Sem_i), syntactic structure (Syn_j) and lexical feature (Lex_k) for a set of input strings ($Words$), and a loss of C_2 if we make a wrong choice. Then the expected cost, based on any scoring mechanism, would be

$$Cost = C_1 \times P(Sem_i, Syn_j, Lex_k | Words)$$
$$+ C_2 \times (1 - P(Sem_i, Syn_j, Lex_k | Words)$$

Since, in general, we will incur small or no loss when we make a right choice, so C_1 can be set zero (or negative). Furthermore, we can think of C_2 as a positive constant corresponding to the extra efforts for post-editing. Under such circumstances, to minimize the cost of disambiguation would be

equivalent to maximizing $P(Sem_i, Syn_j, Lex_k | Words)$, namely to maximize our
score function. Therefore, with the score function as the preference measure,
we will incur *minimal cost*, in *Bayesian* sense, for disambiguation.

7.2.3. Decomposition of Score Function

Now that we have a good sense about the optimality property of the score
function, how can we use this general formula to deal with the general problems
of disambiguation in linguistic level?   In the following sections, we will
briefly outline some possible ways to apply the score function to different
driving mechanisms by decomposing the score function in different ways. In
particular, we will map this function to a Generalized LR parser (GLR parser for
short) which can handle augmented context-free grammars for natural language
processing.

First of all, let's decompose the score function to show how the score function
can be related to traditional *stratified analysis* paradigm. To simplify the analysis
tasks in different analysis phases, we can usually compute a score by dividing
the score function into three components as follows:

$$SCORE(Sem_i, Syn_j, Lex_k, Words)$$
$$\equiv P(Sem_i, Syn_j, Lex_k | w_1 \ldots w_n)$$
$$= P(Sem_i | Syn_j, Lex_k, w_1 \ldots w_n) \times P(Syn_j | Lex_k, w_1 \ldots w_n) \quad (7.1)$$
$$\times P(Lex_k | w_1 \ldots w_n)$$
$$= SCORE_{sem} \times SCORE_{syn} \times SCORE_{lex}$$

where w_1 through w_n are the input words in the given sentence. In this formula,
the three product terms are referred to as *semantic score* ($SCORE_{sem}$), *syntactic
score* ($SCORE_{syn}$) and *lexical score* ($SCORE_{lex}$), respectively. By making such
decomposition, we can model traditional stratified analysis approach easily. In
other words, we can perform lexical analysis, syntax analysis and semantic
analysis based on lexical score, syntactic score and semantic score, respectively.
The total *compositional score* then serves as the global indicator to the degree
of preference of a given interpretation.

For simplicity, we will focus only on the syntactic aspect of this score
function, namely $SCORE_{syn}$, and show how to compute $SCORE_{syn}$ under GLR
parsing environment.   These techniques can be extended to the other two
components of the compositional score function as well. The goal here is to
get the most probable *syntactic structure* when the *input words* and their *lexical
feature* (represented by part of speech) are given. We can first simplify the
above syntactic score function as $SCORE_{syn}(Syn_j) \equiv P(Syn_j | Lex_k | w_1 \ldots w_n) \approx$
$P(Syn_j | Lex_k) = P(Syn_j | c_1 \ldots c_n)$, where c_1 to c_n are the lexical categories (part
of speech) corresponding to w_1 to w_n. In making the simplification, we assume
that the syntactic structure is independent of the terminal strings themselves

but depends on their part of speech. This is usually the case in GLR parsing. After the simplification is made, we can get the score by properly decomposing this formula into pieces of probability entries, which can then be evaluated stepwise through the process of GLR parsing. In the following sections, two such formulations for syntactic score are proposed to show the versatility of the score function.

7.2.4. Syntactic Score in Context Sensitive Model

To show the mechanism for computing syntactic score informally, first refer to the syntax tree in Figure 7.1. The syntax tree is decomposed into a number of *phrase levels*, each phrase level being a set of symbols (terminal or nonterminal) which can derive all the terminal symbols in a sentence. The phrase levels shown here correspond to a canonical derivation sequence which is produced by a generalized LR bottom-up parsing algorithm. Let L_i be the i-th phrase level. Then a transition from phrase level L_{i+1} to phrase level L_i corresponds to a *derivation* of a nonterminal at time t_i. On the other hand, transition from L_i to L_{i+1} would be equivalent to a *reduction* at t_i.

After the syntax tree is decomposed into phrase levels, we can express the syntactic score in terms of these phrase levels. For example, the syntactic score of the syntax tree in Figure 7.1 can be formulated as the following conditional probability equation, where l_i and r_i are the left and right contexts of the symbols to be reduced:

$$
\begin{aligned}
SCORE_{syn}&(Syn_A) \\
&= P(L_8, L_7 \ldots L_2 | L_1) \\
&= P(L_8 | L_7 \ldots L_2, L_1) \times P(L_7 | L_6 \ldots L_1) \times \cdots P(L_2 | L_1) \\
&\approx P(L_8 | L_7) \times P(L_7 | L_6) \times \cdots \times P(L_2 | L_1) \\
&\approx P(\{A\} | \{l_7, B, C, r_7\}) \times P(\{C\} | \{l_6, F, G, r_6\}) \times \cdots \\
&\quad \times P(\{D\} | \{l_1, c_1, r_1\})
\end{aligned}
\tag{7.2}
$$

Note that the product terms in the last formula correspond to the *rightmost derivation* sequence in a GLR parser with left and right contexts taken into account. Therefore, such formulation is especially useful for generalized LR parsing algorithm in which context-sensitive processing power is desirable. The degree of context-sensitivity is specified by the number of context symbols to be consulted. This number is called the *order* of context-sensitivity of the score function.

If the order of context-sensitivity for left and right contexts are m and n respectively, it is said to operate in *LmRn* mode. For example, Equation (7.2)

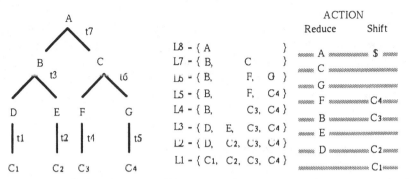

Figure 7.1. Decomposition of a syntax tree into phrase levels for score computation in bottum-up GLR parsing.

can be further reduced to the following equation when operating in L1R1 mode:

$$SCORE_{syn}(Syn_A)$$
$$\approx P(\{A\}|\{\emptyset, B, C\emptyset\}) \times P(\{C\}|\{B, F, G, \emptyset\}) \times \cdots \qquad (7.3)$$
$$\times P(\{D\}|\{\emptyset, c_1, c_2\})$$

where "$\emptyset$" is the null symbol. In this case, only one immediate context symbol, either to the left or to the right of the reduced symbols, is consulted.

Some systems (especially those dealing with spoken language processing) have tried to adopt L0R0 mode of operation in probabilistic parsing. In this case, the languages are assumed to be fully context-free, and a probability (or certainty factor) is assigned to each production rule. The score is then computed as the product of these probability entries. As we can see from the above equation, this mode of operation is a highly simplified operation mode. As the structural and contextual information of the language become more and more important, this mode of operation will become less feasible. To improve the system performance under such circumstances, one can follow the above formulation and increase the order of context-sensitivity of the score function.

7.2.5. Syntactic Score in Run-Time Model

The formulation for syntactic score computation in Equations (7.2) and (7.3) can take place when the parser is executing a **reduce** action. We shall now show another alternative in which the computation takes place when a **shift** action is executed.

In GLR parsing, we may wish the computation of scores to occur after an input word is just fetched. This is often the case in *parallel* parsing algorithms (such as parallel truncation algorithm and Tomita's algorithm [Tomi 87]) where a number of paths are compared based on the partial cumulative scores of the *same* input subsentence (or more exactly, based on the same *prefix*).

This can be done by compacting multiple **reduce** actions and a single **shift** into one step and formulate the syntactic score $SCORE_{syn}(Syn_A)$ as follows.

$$
\begin{aligned}
SCORE_{syn}&(Syn_A) \\
&= P(L_8, L_7 \ldots L_2 | L_1) \\
&= P(L_8, L_7, L_6 | L_5, L_4 \ldots L_1) \times P(L_5 | L_4, L_3 \ldots L_1) \\
&\quad \times P(L_4, L_3 | L_2) \times P(L_2 | L_1) \\
&\approx P(L_8, L_7, L_6 | L_5) \times P(L_5 | L_4) \times P(L_4, L_3 | L_2) \times P(L_2 | L_1) \\
&\approx P(L_8 | L_5) \times P(L_5 | L_4) \times P(L_4 | L_2) \times P(L_2 | L_1)
\end{aligned}
\tag{7.4}
$$

The probability entries in the last simplified formula correspond to a sequence of change in the *stack contents* between two **shifts**. In fact, the stack contents immediately after c_1, c_2, c_3, c_4 and $\$$ (the end-of-sentence symbol) are pushed onto the stack are $\{c_1, (c_2, c_3, c_4, \$)\}$, $\{D, c_2, (c_3, c_4, \$)\}$, $\{B, F, c_4, (\$)\}$, and $\{A, ()\}$, which are the *prefix* of L_1, L_2, L_4, L_5 and L_8, respectively. (The terminal symbols in the parentheses are the input symbols not yet fetched.) Such formulation makes run-time score computation an easy task because we can simply monitor the status of the stack and compute the probability entries step-by-step after an input word is shifted.

Two assumptions were made in formulating Equations (7.2) – (7.4). First, it is assumed that the formation of phrase level i is only dependent on its immediate lower phrase level, since most information percolated from other lower levels is contained in that level. And second, a reduction or derivation is only locally context sensitive to its immediate left or right context at each phrase level. This assumption is also supported in other systems as well [Marc 80, Gars 87].

7.2.6. Brief Summary

From the previous sections, it is easy to see that the whole scoring mechanism consists of three main components:

1. *score function* which defines the preference measure of a given interpretation.
2. Different types of *decomposition schemes* which apply the score function to different driving mechanisms or algorithms in different mode.
3. A *simplification scheme* to simplify the computation for each decomposition scheme, which also determines the order of context-sensitivity.

We have introduced only two decomposition schemes in the previous sections. The versatility of this scoring mechanism, however, is beyond what we have described here. For more information about other formulations and the comparison to other probabilistic models in the wide variety of linguistic levels, interested readers can refer to [Su 90] for more formal description.

With such score function, we can extend the power of a context free grammar to any degree of context-sensitivity (in probabilistic sense), depending on the number of context symbols to be consulted. Such extension is quite different

from other *trainable grammar* like [Bake 79], where N-gram paradigm is used
to train a context-free grammar with restricted (and hence unnatural) right hand
side symbols. Under our score function paradigm, the grammar rules can be
any augmented context-free grammar written by linguists, and the contextual
information is embedded in the statistic knowledge of the score function (and
other augmentation not mentioned here). The score function thus integrates
linguistic reality and statistic knowledge in an elegant way.

A simulation based solely on the *syntactic score* was conducted and reported
in [Su 88a] with a full-path searching algorithm. The result shows that the
correct syntactic structures of over 85% of the test sentences were successfully
ranked at the *first* place when a total of 3 local left and right context symbols
were consulted. In addition, over 93% of the correct syntax trees are ranked at
the *first* or *second* place based on the syntactic score with 2 context symbols.
With *semantic score* incorporated into the mechanism, the results should be even
more promising.

7.3. The Sequential Truncation Algorithm

7.3.1. Basic Algorithm

Using the score function defined in the previous section, we will present the
idea of sequential truncation algorithm with Figure 7.2.

Each path in Figure 7.2 corresponds to a possible derivation of a given
sentence. The parser will traverse the searching tree with the depth-first strategy.
But during the searching process, the parser compares the accumulated running
score of each path with a running threshold constant $C(\alpha_i)$ at each step i when
the i-th word is fetched. If the score of the path is less than the running threshold
$C(\alpha_i)$, it will be truncated, i.e. blocked, and the next path will be tried. This
process continues until we get the complete parse tree. The fraction of paths to
be blocked at each step is determined by the control variable α_i which will be
defined later in the next section.

After we obtain the first complete parse tree, a lower bound for the scores,
initially set to the score of the first parse tree, is also acquired. The parser will
continue to traverse other paths, but from now on, the score of each path will
also be compared with the current low bound for the scores in addition to be
compared with the running threshold. This additional comparison is similar to
the *branch and bound* strategy employed in AI applications [Wins 84] and it
will accelerate the parsing process further. If the test fails in either case, this
path will be truncated. Continuing in this manner, we will update the lower
bound whenever a new complete parse tree has a score higher than current
lower bound, and repeat the whole process until the end of the entire searching
process. The whole process is shown in the flow chart in Figure 7.3.

When all the paths are blocked without arriving at any complete parse tree,

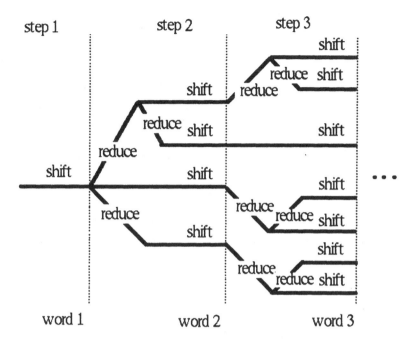

Figure 7.2. The searching tree.

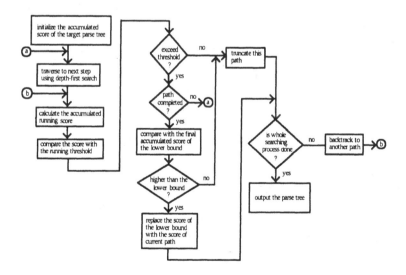

Figure 7.3. Flow chart for sequential truncation parsing algorithm.

we can adopt one of two possible strategies. First, we could loosen the running thresholds, i.e. lowering $C(\alpha_i)$, and try the deepest path gone so far again. Second, we can process this sentence in *fail-soft* mode. The fail-soft mechanism will skip and discard the current state and attempt to continue the parsing at some later point.

As we can see, the score of each syntax tree can be expressed as the product of a sequence of conditional probabilities such as the one shown in Equation (7.4). Each term in the product corresponds to a transition between two **shift** actions and is evaluated immediately after a **shift**. To avoid mathematical underflow, we shall take the logarithm on both sides of Equation (7.4) to get a logarithmic score in the form of:

$$\log(SCORE_{syn}(Syn)) = \sum_{i=1}^{L} \log P(X'_i|X_i) \qquad (7.5)$$

where L is the length of the sentence, X_i denotes the set of phrase levels which have been encountered up to the i-th **shift**, and X'_i is the complement of X_i, namely the set of phrase levels not yet encountered up to the i-th **shift**.

7.3.2. Analytic Description

The effectiveness of the sequential truncation algorithm is closely related to the distribution of scores of the database and the distribution of scores of the input sentences. This phenomenon will be illustrated in the following paragraphs.

If we define $y_j \equiv \sum_{i=1}^{j} \log P(X'_i|X_i)$, then y_j is the accumulated logarithmic score up to the j-th word, which is also the accumulated score after the j-th **shift** of the sentence.

Suppose we have M sentences with their correct parse trees in the database. For each parse tree, we can evaluate y_j by using the logarithmic score function defined in Equation (7.5). So for the k-th sentence in the database, we obtain a sequence $y_1^k, y_2^k, \ldots, y_{L_k}^k$, where y_j^k is the accumulated logarithmic score of the k-th sentence up to the j-th step, and L_k is the length of the k-th sentence.

Given these accumulative scores found in the database, we can define a set of random variables Y_i corresponding to y_i^k, with k ranged from 1 to M. In other words, Y_i is the random variable corresponding to the accumulative logarithmic scores up to the i-th word of the sentences in the database. Using the samples in the database, we can draw a histogram for each Y_i and approximate each histogram by a continuous density function $f_Y^i(y)$.

To allow a fraction α_i, say 99%, of the best parse trees in the database to pass the threshold test at step i, we can set a constant $C(\alpha_i)$ such that $P(Y_i \geq C(\alpha_i)) = \alpha_i$, where $C(\alpha_i)$ is the running threshold that we will use to compare with the running accumulated logarithmic score at step i. Those paths with running accumulated logarithmic score y_i less than $C(\alpha_i)$

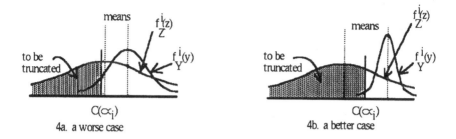

Figure 7.4. Relationship between the running score of the input text and the cumulative score of the database

would be blocked at the i-th step. Using the notation defined above, the probability of obtaining the desired parse tree for a sentence with length L_k would be $\prod_{i=1}^{L_k} \alpha_i$.

For the input sentences to be parsed, we can also define a set of random variables Z_i corresponding to the distribution of the accumulated logarithmic scores at the i-th step and a set of density function $f_Z^i(z)$ associated with Z_i. These probability entries would be evaluated from the ambiguous trees of the input sentences. Figure 7.4 shows the relationship between the probability density function $f_Z^i(z)$ (the distribution of the i-th running score of the *input text*) and the probability density function $f_Y^i(y)$ (the distribution of cumulative score of the *database*.) In the figure, the dashed lines indicate the means of the two density functions. Since the step-wise cumulative scores in the database are evaluated using the correct parse trees in the database, we would expect that the expectation of Y_i is greater than that of Z_i and the variance of Y_i is less than that of Z_i. In other words, we have $E[Y_i] > E[Z_i]$ and $\mathrm{Var}[Y_i] < \mathrm{Var}[Z_i]$ in normal situation.

Let β_i denote $F_Z^i(C(\alpha_i))$, where F_Z^i is the cumulated distribution function of Z_i, then β_i is the probability that a path will be truncated at the i-th step of the searching process. By using this sequential truncation method, the searching space would then be approximately reduced to $\prod_{i=1}^{L_k}(1 - \beta_i)$, which is a small portion of the original searching space generated by a full path searching algorithm. Therefore the efficiency of parsing is increased. Since β_i in Figure 7.4a is less than that in Figure 7.4b, which correspond to the situation that has a large expectation difference ($E[Y_i] - E[Z_i]$) and a small variance ratio ($\mathrm{Var}[Y_i]/\mathrm{Var}[Z_i]$), the underlying grammar that has the property of Figure 7.4b would benefit most from this algorithm. In addition, we can see that if we increase the running threshold $C(\alpha_i)$, we will get a greater β_i and a lower α_i. The parsing efficiency will thus increase, but the probability (i.e. $\prod_{i=1}^{L_k} \alpha_i$) that we will get the desired parse tree would decrease. How to select a good $C(\alpha_i)$

to achieve a desired success rate is thus very important. In the following section, this issue would be discussed in greater details.

7.4. How To Set The Running Threshold

7.4.1. Static Running Threshold

Using the model given in the last section, the probability that we will get the global optimal solution, i.e. the parse tree with the largest score, for a sentence of length L is $K_L = \prod_{i=1}^{L} \alpha_i$, where K_L is a constant *pre-selected* by the system designer as a compromise between the parsing *efficiency* and the translation *quality*. Assuming that the average branching factor for each path is a constant N, then the average total number of paths we have to try is:

$$
\begin{aligned}
g(\alpha_1 \ldots \alpha_L) &= N + N \times (1 - \beta_1) \times N \\
&\quad + N \times (1 - \beta_1) \times N \times (1 - \beta_2) \times Nt \cdots \\
&= N \times (1 + N \times h(\alpha_1) + N^2 \times h(\alpha_1) \times h(\alpha_2) + \cdots) \\
&= N \times \left(1 + \sum_{i=1}^{L-1} N^i \times \prod_{j=1}^{i} h(\alpha_j) \right)
\end{aligned}
\tag{7.6}
$$

where $h(\alpha_i) \equiv (1 - \beta_i)$. In order to minimize the path number, we must have $h(\alpha_1) < h(\alpha_2) < \cdots < h(\alpha_L)$ because $h(\alpha_i)$ has more significant influence on the number of paths to be truncated than $h(\alpha_{i+1})$.

The problem of selecting an appropriate running threshold $C(\alpha_i)$ is now converted into one of minimizing $g(\alpha_1 \ldots \alpha_L)$ under the constraint of $\prod_{i=1}^{L} \alpha_i = K_L$. Taking the logarithm on both sides, we get $\sum_{i=1}^{L} \log \alpha_i = \log K_L$. Then the *Lagrange multiplier* λ is introduced to get $g^*(\alpha_1 \ldots \alpha_L) = g(\alpha_1 \ldots \alpha_L) + \lambda * \sum_{i=1}^{L} \log \alpha_i$. Taking the partial derivative of g^* with respect to $\alpha_1 \ldots \alpha_L$, we will get the following simultaneous equations:

$$
\frac{\partial g^*}{\partial \alpha_1} = 0, \quad \frac{\partial g^*}{\partial \alpha_2} = 0, \quad \ldots \quad \frac{\partial g^*}{\partial \alpha_L} = 0, \quad \text{and}
$$

$$
\sum_{i=1}^{L} \log \alpha_i = \log K_L
\tag{7.7}
$$

In the above equations, there are $(L + 1)$ variables, which are $\alpha_1 \ldots \alpha_L$, and λ, and $(L + 1)$ equations. So, $\alpha_1 \ldots \alpha_L$ can be solved by a numerical method. Since α_i is usually very close to 1, we can linearize the function $h(\alpha_i)$ in the region around $\alpha_i = 1$ and approximate it by $h(\alpha_i) \approx a \times \alpha_i + b$. In this way, we can substitute $h(\alpha_i)$ in the above equation by $a \times \alpha_i + b$ to simplify the calculation.

During our derivation, we have assumed that the average branching factor at each stage is a constant N. This constraint can be relaxed by assuming the average branching factor at the i-th stage to be N_i. In this way, we will get a more complicated expression for $g(\alpha_i \ldots \alpha_L)$, but it can still be solved in the same way.

The running threshold $C(\alpha_i)$ can now be computed off-line by selecting different K_L for different sentence length L. We will call this set of $C(\alpha_i)$ the *static* running threshold, because once they are computed, they will not be changed during the parsing process.

7.4.2. Dynamic Running Threshold

The static threshold derived in the above section can serve as a limiting factor in the truncation algorithm. However, if we arrive at a complete parse tree with much higher final accumulated running score than the final accumulated running threshold, then the running threshold should be adjusted to reflect the higher final accumulated running score. Such adjustment is necessary because even if a path can pass all the threshold tests it might still be discarded when compared with the much higher final accumulated running score. Therefore, it would be better if the running threshold is changed to $C'(\alpha_i) = c(\alpha_i) + \Delta C(\alpha_i)$, where $\Delta C(\alpha_i)$ is set to $\gamma \times (y_i^* - C(\alpha_i))$, $0 \leq \gamma \leq 1$, and y_i^* is the accumulated score of the current best parse tree at the i-th step. The tunning constant γ is another control variable pre-selected by the system designer. Since $C'(\alpha_i)$ is adjusted dynamically it will be called the *dynamic* running threshold. Using the dynamic running threshold, the efficiency of parsing would be further improved.

If it so happen that all paths are blocked before a complete parse tree is formed, we can find the deepest path (assuming it to be at the j-th step) among the blocked ones, and reactivate it with a lowered running threshold of $C'(\alpha_j) = y_j'$, where y_j' is the score of this path at the j-th step. Since the procedure to lower the running threshold is quite complicated it might be more convenient just to invoke the fail-soft mechanism for sentences whose paths are all blocked.

7.5. Scored Truncation vs Charted Parsing

It is interesting to make a comparison between the well-known chart mechanism [Wino 83] and the truncation algorithm. In many current systems, a chart-like approach is used to accelerate the parsing speed by avoiding the reparsing overhead of substructures which had been constructed previously. In the previous sections, we have demonstrated the speedup effects of the scored sequential truncation algorithm, which accelerates parsing speed by cutting down the searching space with the aids of a good scoring function. Is it profitable to combine these two mechanisms into one? The answer seems to be "yes" if the parsing *speed* is the only concern.

Nevertheless, there is a few words to be said about the combination of these

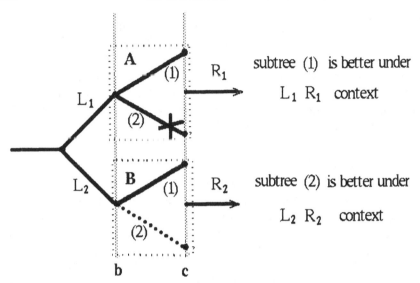

subtree (1) is better under

$L_1\ R_1$ context

subtree (2) is better under

$L_2\ R_2$ context

Figure 7.5. Chart with truncation mechanism.

two mechanisms. When the truncation algorithm is adopted in a chart parser, the best tree originally selected by a chart parser might not appear in the trees produced by its truncation version. This phenomenon lies in the fact that *chart* mechanism is essentially in conflict with the *truncation* mechanism in their operations. The reason for having chart is to be able to *retain* all subtrees that were parsed in previous path traversal. So, when we backtrack to the next path and arrive at the same set of input strings, the same subtrees can be used again without reparsing. On the contrary, the idea behind the truncation mechanism is to *discard* a subtree which has low score as early as possible. Therefore, if we adopt the truncation mechanism during charted parsing, not every possible subtree between a set of input words will be successfully constructed and stored into the chart. For example, in Figure 7.5, there are two possible subtrees between *b* and *c*. When the paths in block A are expanded, one of the subtrees is discarded while the other is stored into the chart.

The subtree may be discarded for the following two reasons. First, it might be due to the semantic constraints on the contextual dependency of the system. Second, the subtree might be discarded because of its small running accumulated score (and thus truncated by the truncation mechanism). Either will leave us a chart with incomplete subchart. So, this might result in the best possible tree being missed as a side-effect of using this chart under other contextual environment. For instance, the best tree in Figure 7.5 might consist of the second subtree, the left context L_2, and the right context R_2. But, since the path expansion starting from the left context L_1 has the second subtree discarded because of its low score under the context of L_1 and R_1, the best tree will never be formed. Therefore, with a chart having incomplete subcharts, the possibility of obtaining the best tree might be affected by the paths truncated before.

One solution to this incompatibility problem is to mark the subcharts as being complete or incomplete. If an incomplete subchart is encountered again, it will be reparsed. On the other hand, if a complete set of chart is encountered, the subtrees can be copied directly from the chart. Another solution is to suspend the truncation mechanism when a chart is being tried the first time. And if subtrees are copied directly from the chart, the truncation mechanism resumes its normal operation. In this way, it is guaranteed that every subchart in the chart is complete. Both of these solutions will introduce some overhead. This compromise, however, is unavoidable if the advantages of using chart are to be retained.

7.6. Testing

We have completed two preliminary tests on the truncation algorithm with two special versions of our English-Chinese MT system, the ARCHTRAN. These two tests use a database which contains the required probability entries acquired from a set of 1430 sentences. A more extended test based on a database of 1607 sentences is also conducted. The following paragraphs will describe these tests in detail.

In the first experiment, the parsing time needed by a *chart parser* is compared with the time needed by the same chart parser which is augmented with *truncation* mechanism. The chart parser adopted a *bottom-up parsing with top-down filtering* strategy (TD+BU for short, see [Su 87a]). Its parsing efficiency is about the same order as Tomita's extended chart parser [Tomi 87, Su 89] and it has a mean speed-up factor of about 43 over traditional uncharted LR parser. From the test, we found that the average parsing time by the chart parser with truncation is improved by a factor of about 4. For some sentences, the improvement can go as high as a factor of 20. This result is encouraging.

In the second experiment, we converted the chart parser for the first experiment into a chartless one. Similar test is conducted for this chartless parser but with a smaller analysis grammar. The result shows that the total parsing time for this parser with truncation mechanism added is better than the same parser without truncation by a factor of about 3. Because the uncharted parsers are relatively more slower than the previous charted ones, only a few sentences are tested which account for the above speedup factor.

In the previous two tests, the size of the test samples is small. A more extended test was conducted with even more encouraging results. The results, together with a sentence length distribution curve, are shown in Figure 7.6. More detailed test data is listed in the Appendix of this chapter. In the test, two parsers

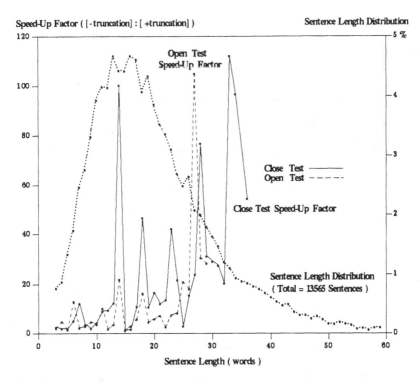

Figure 7.6. Comparison between the speeds of truncation parser and non-truncation parser.

were used to show the effects of *sequential truncation* algorithm with respect to *charted parsing*. The first parser is a TD+BU chart parser, which does not adopt truncation algorithm. The second parser is a truncation-based bottom-up (BU) parser, which does not use chart mechanism. The score database for the second parser contains 1607 sentences which are decomposed into probability entries in L2R1 format (that is, 2 left context symbols and 1 right lookahead are consulted). The augmented context-free grammar used in the test contains a set of 1046 production rules. Under such test environment and taking the sentence length distribution into account, the mean speed-up factor for a set of 165 sentences from inside the database is about 17 (close test). For another set of test data which contains 196 sentences from outside the database, the speed-up factor is about 9 (open test). In general, the speed-up factors vary with the number of ambiguity and the length of the sentences. (Individual comparison shows speed-up factors ranging from 1 to more than 100 in both open and close tests.) Nevertheless, the figure shows a tendency of increasing speed-up factors with length (and hence with structural complexity) of the sentences. This tendency is very encouraging because a truncation algorithm is most beneficial for long sentences in which a large number of paths can be cut down.

In the above tests, only *syntactic* score and *static* threshold were used. We expect that more searching space will be cut down and hence larger speed-up factors will result when *semantic* score and *dynamic* running threshold are incorporated into the truncation algorithm. From the positive results of the above experiments, we have shown the inclusion of the sequential truncation algorithm is advantageous for a MT system.

7.7. Concluding Remarks

In an operational machine translation system, it is important to arrive at a *good* analysis for a sentence in a *reasonably short time*. One way to achieve this is to decrease the parsing time by reducing the searching space. We have proposed a *sequential truncation* algorithm with a *score function* to achieve this goal. There are several reasons for adopting this strategy. First, the first parse tree with a moderate quality can be found quickly and easily. Second, the running threshold serves to truncate part of the paths that is quite unlikely to lead to the best analysis, and thus greatly reduces the searching space.

The optimality property of the score function has been described in this chapter. Some possible decomposition schemes for tailoring this function to a GLR parser are also introduced. In particular, we have shown how to model the stratified analysis paradigm with the score function, and demonstrated the versatility of the score function by introducing two decomposition schemes about the syntactic score.

In the sequential truncation strategy, a sequence of running thresholds are used to bound the searching space during each step of the scored parsing process. Additional speedup can be acquired by a branch-and-bound strategy if the accumulated score for a parse is lower than a dynamically adjusted lower bound.

We have pointed out the incompatibility problem between the use of *chart* and the *truncation* mechanism. As our current research topic, we shall resolve the incompatibility problem between the chart mechanism and the truncation algorithm, and include the solution into our working MT system, the ARCHTRAN.

We have made a pilot test on the truncation mechanism with a chart parser that adopts bottom-up parsing with top-down filtering strategy. With a database of 1430 sentences, the result indicates an average improvement in the parsing time by a factor of 4 (for some sentences the improvement goes as high as a factor of 20). In another pilot test on the truncation mechanism, the parsing time is tested for a chartless parser that adopts sequential parsing strategy. The result shows an improvement in parsing time by a factor of 3 for the inclusion of the truncation mechanism. These encouraging results demonstrate a great promise for the sequential truncation strategy. In another extended test, we have achieved mean speed-up factors of 9 and 17 for open test and close test, respectively. This result shows a great improvement of the sequential truncation algorithm over conventional chart parser if a good score function is available.

Appendix: Open Test and Close Test

The following tables show the results of the open and close tests described in the chapter (see also Figure 7.6). The environment under which the tests were conducted is summarized as follows:

- Parser #1: [−Truncation] [+Chart] [TD+BU]
- Parser #2: [+Truncation] [−Chart] [BU] (Bottom Up)
- Score Data Base: 1607 sentences (L2R1)
- Grammar: 1046 production rules
- Open Test: 196 sentences (executed at SUN-4/260)
- Close Test: 165 sentences (executed at SUN-4/110)
- Mean Speed-Up: Open Test = 9 & Close Test = 17

References

[Bake 79] Baker, J.K., "Trainable Grammars for Speech Recognition," *Proc. of the Spring Conf. of the Acoustical Society of America*, 1979.

[Benn 85] Bennett, W.S. and J. Slocum, "The LRC Machine Translation System," *Computational Linguistics*, vol. 11, no. 2–3, pp. 111–119, ACL, Apr.-Sep. 1985.

[Chia 89] Chiang, T.-H., *The Design of a Chinese Phonetic Typewriter*, Master thesis, National Tsing Hua University, Hsinchu, TAIWAN, R.O.C., 1989.

[Gars 87] Garside, Roger, Geoffrey Leech and Geoffrey Sampson (eds.), *The Computational Analysis of English : A Corpus-Based Approach*, Longman , New York, 1987.

[Marc 80] Marcus, M.P., *A Theory of Syntactic Recognition for Natural Language*, MIT Press, Cambridge, MA, 1980.

[Robi 82] Robinson, J.J., "DIAGRAM : A Grammar for Dialogues," *CACM*, vol. 25, no. 1, pp. 27–47, ACM, Jan. 1982.

[Su 87a] Su, K.-Y., J.-S. Chang, and H.-H. Hsu, "A Powerful Language Processing System for English-Chinese Machine Translation," *Proc. of 1987 Int. Conf. on Chinese and Oriental Language Computing*, pp.260–264, Chicago, Ill., USA, 1987.

[Su 87b] Su, K.-Y., J.-N. Wang, W.-H. Li, and J.-S. Chang, "A New Parsing Strategy in Natural Language Processing Based on the Truncation Algorithm", *Proc. of Natl. Computer Symposium (NCS)*, pp. 580–586, Taipei, Taiwan. 1987.

[Su 88a] Su, K.-Y. and J.-S.Chang, "Semantic and Syntactic Aspects of Score Function," *Proc. COLING-88*, vol. 2, pp. 642–644, 12th Int. Conf. on Comput. Linguistics, Budapest, Hungary, 22–27 Aug. 1988.

[Su 88b] Su, K.-Y., "Principles and Techniques of Natural Language Parsing : A Tutorial," *Proc. of ROCLING-I*, pp.57–61, Nantou, Taiwan. Oct. 1988.

[Su 89] Su, K.-Y. and J.-S. Chang, "Some Key Issues in Designing Machine Translation Systems," (submitted), 1989.

[Su 90] Su, K.-Y., J.-S. Chang and Y.-C. Lin, "A Unified Approach to Disambiguation Using A Uniform Formulation of Probabilistic Score Functions," (to appear), 1990.

[Tomi 87] Tomita, M., "An Efficient Augmented-Context-Free Parsing Algorithm," *Computational Linguistics*, vol. 13, no. 1–2, pp. 31–46, 1987.

Table 7.1. *Close test*

Length (words)	No. of test sentences	1st parser total CPU time (sec)	2nd parser total CPU time (sec)	Speed-up (1st/2nd)
3	2	2.85	1.09	2.61
4	2	5.81	2.92	1.99
5	2	2.63	1.37	1.92
6	2	31.62	6.12	5.17
7	2	33.99	2.72	12.27
8	2	19.60	5.38	3.64
9	2	15.31	7.80	1.96
10	5	175.86	39.50	4.45
11	5	518.89	56.93	9.11
12	4	387.64	40.74	9.51
13	3	448.02	36.33	12.33
14	5	3647.54	86.29	42.27
15	3	143.51	125.65	1.14
16	6	300.34	175.57	1.71
17	11	1950.57	237.51	8.21
18	12	16901.77	360.53	46.88
19	13	4882.46	448.87	10.88
20	18	13148.05	785.17	16.75
21	14	11560.29	957.19	12.08
22	12	7624.84	560.50	13.60
23	9	33879.85	801.12	42.29
24	6	6377.89	292.22	21.83
25	2	407.79	138.53	2.94
26	3	1534.79	97.97	15.67
27	3	8949.71	370.90	24.13
28	2	6651.16	86.40	76.98
29	3	4236.36	135.33	31.30
30	3	2444.76	83.89	29.14
31	2	1749.56	63.50	27.55
32	2	2881.16	140.11	20.56
33	2	8471.91	75.48	112.24
34	2	15669.64	161.78	96.86
36	1	2533.35	46.48	54.50
TOTAL	165	157589.52	6431.94	24.50
MEAN (take sentence length distribution into account)				17.22

[Wino 83] Winograd, Terry, *Language as a Cognitive Process*, Addison-Wesley, Reading, MA., USA, 1983.

[Wins 84] Winston, P.H., *Artificial Intelligence*, Addison-Wesley, Reading, MA., USA, 1984.

Table 7.2. *Open test*

Length (words)	No. of test sentences	1st Parser Total CPU Time (sec)	2nd Parser Total CPU Time (sec)	Speed-Up (1st/2nd)
3	4	3.70	1.76	2.10
4	5	7.29	1.50	4.86
5	5	6.31	3.99	1.58
6	5	61.88	4.73	13.08
7	9	39.12	16.62	2.35
8	10	79.52	27.17	2.93
9	10	315.52	67.75	4.66
10	10	266.15	73.72	3.61
11	9	377.72	36.81	10.26
12	9	154.69	81.72	1.89
13	10	359.94	128.87	2.79
14	9	2779.25	126.72	21.93
15	8	179.15	137.21	1.31
16	9	587.23	198.93	2.95
17	8	2121.77	358.72	5.91
18	9	5391.85	328.23	16.43
19	10	1814.09	385.68	4.70
20	11	4888.94	807.30	6.06
21	14	8916.45	1217.73	7.32
22	8	1104.86	406.98	2.71
23	4	1238.93	162.71	7.61
24	4	2249.22	268.99	8.36
25	3	1905.49	90.29	21.10
26	4	10292.94	563.95	18.25
27	2	8759.70	83.29	105.17
28	1	677.92	22.07	30.72
29	6	5969.74	209.76	28.46
TOTAL	196	60549.37	5813.20	10.42
MEAN (take sentence length distribution into account)				9.07

8 GLR Parsing With Probability

J. H. Wright and E. N. Wrigley

8.1. Introduction

Structured recursive hierarchical models such as context-free grammars have applications in many areas and the attractions of the LR parsing strategy are such that generalisations which enable this strategy to be employed in new areas should be warmly welcomed by many researchers. An area of particular interest to us is the recognition of continuous speech and it was with this application in mind that the probabilistic LR parser was developed. However, there are likely to be other applications as well, perhaps in handwriting and optical character recognition and in certain compilers.

The LR parser described in this chapter, which builds upon the Tomita algorithm [1,2], is applicable when

1. the grammar production rules have associated probabilities, and
2. the input string is uncertain.

Quite apart from the possibility of ambiguity in the grammar, the input uncertainty allows there to be a number of sentences (and therefore of parses) compatible with both the grammar and the input data. The algorithm recursively computes the probability of each possible parse, given all the data up to the m'th word, from the parse probabilities up to the (m-1)'th word and the latest data. At the end of the sentence the parse probabilities allow the most likely interpretation to be adopted with a backup of progressively less likely alternatives if required.

The starting-point is a "probabilistic context-free grammar (PCFG)" [3-5]. This is a 4-tuple $\langle N, T, R, S \rangle$ where N is a nonterminal vocabulary including the start symbol S, T is a terminal vocabulary, and R is a set of production-rules each of which is a pair of form $\langle A \to \alpha, p \rangle$, with $A \in N$, $\alpha \in (N \cup T)^*$, and p a probability. The probabilities associated with all the rules having a particular nonterminal on the LHS must sum to one. A probability is associated with each derivation by multiplying the probabilities of those rules used, in keeping with the context-freeness of the grammar.

A very simple PCFG can be seen in Figure 8.1: the symbols in uppercase are the nonterminals, those in lowercase are the terminals (actually preterminals) and λ denotes the null string.

We shall assume that the elements of the terminal vocabulary T can be written as $a, \ldots, a_{|T|}$ and that one of them is identified with an end-of-sentence marker

(1) S → NP VP, 1.0	(3) REL → pron VP, 0.3
(2) NP → pn, 0.4	(6) VP → iv, 0.5
(3) NP → det n REL, 0.6	(7) VP → tv NP, 0.5
(4) REL → λ, 0.7	

Figure 8.1. A simple probabilistic grammer.

$. At several points we shall also refer to a small threshold probability ϵ, mainly used to prune out improbable alternatives.

Section 8.2 contains the theory of the parser generator for the three common kinds of LR parser: SLR, canonical, and LALR. Section 8.3 contains the algorithm for dealing with the input uncertainty and some complexity issues are considered in Section 8.4.

8.2. LR Parsing for Probabilistic CFGs

The LR parsing strategy can be applied to a PCFG if the rule-probabilities are driven down into the parsing action table by the parser generator. Ambiguity, left-recursion and null rules are all acceptable. The parser provides a set of prior probabilities for possible next words at successive stages in the recognition of a sentence. The use of these prior probabilities will be described in Section 8.3.1.

8.2.1. SLR Parser

The first aspect of parser construction is the closure function. Suppose that I is an SLR kernel set consisting of LR(0) items of the form

$$\langle A \rightarrow \alpha \cdot \beta, p \rangle$$

The item probability p can be thought of as a posterior probability of the item given the terminal string up to that point. The computation of closure(I) requires that items

$$\langle B \rightarrow \cdot \gamma_r, p_B p_r \rangle$$

be added to the set for each rule $\langle B \rightarrow \gamma_r, p_r \rangle$ with B on the LHS, provided $p_B p_r$ exceeds some small probability threshold ϵ, where p_B is the total of the probabilities of items with B appearing after the dot (in the closed set), which is easily obtained recursively starting from the kernel.

There is a problem with left-recursive grammars in that starting from an item of the form

$$\langle A \rightarrow \alpha \cdot B\beta, p \rangle$$

in the kernel we may after a while derive an item of the form

$$\langle C \rightarrow \cdot B\gamma, pq \rangle$$

for some $q < 1$, and hence $\langle C \rightarrow \cdot B\gamma, pq^2 \rangle$, $\langle C \rightarrow \cdot B\gamma, pq^3 \rangle$ and so on, the total "probability" of this item eventually totalling $p/(1 - q)$ which may exceed one, in which case p_B will also exceed one. To expand on this, suppose that

$$p_{BB} = \sum_\alpha P(B \stackrel{+}{\rightarrow} B\alpha)$$

is the total probability of all left-recursive derivations of B, so that

$$p_{B\#} = 1 - p_{BB}$$

is the "exit" probability from this nonterminal. Then the actual probability associated with an item with B after the dot is not the nominal figure p but $pp_{B\#}$, because this is the probability that this item occurs as the last with B after the dot in the branch leading to the next leaf. This applies equally to kernel and non-kernel items. The total probability of B is therefore $p_B p_{B\#}$ (and is never greater than one). For a non-left-recursive grammar, $p_{B\#} = 1$ for all nonterminals, and for a left-recursive grammar the factor $p_{B\#}$ always cancels out in the development of the algorithm. For the rest of this chapter, therefore, $p_{B\#}$ will be ignored and p and p_B will be referred to as the item and nonterminal "probabilities" respectively.

New kernel sets are generated from a closed set of items by the goto function. If all the items with symbol $X \in (N \cup T)$ after the dot in a set I are

$$\langle A_k \rightarrow \alpha_k \cdot X\beta_k, p_k \rangle \quad \text{for } k = 1, \dots, n,$$
$$\text{with } p_X = \sum_{k=1}^{n_X} p_k$$

then the new kernel set corresponding to X is

$$\{\langle A \rightarrow \alpha_k X \cdot \beta_k, p_k/p_X \rangle \quad \text{for } k = 1, \dots, n_X\}$$

and goto(I, X) is the closure of this set. The set already exists if there is another set which has the same number of elements, an exact counterpart for each dotted item, and a probability for each item that differs from that for its counterpart in the new set by at most ϵ.

Starting from an initial state I_0 consisting of the closure of

$$\{\langle S' \rightarrow \cdot S, 1 \rangle\}$$

where S' is an auxiliary start symbol, this process continues until no further sets are created. They can then be listed as $I_0, I_1, \dots$.

Each state set I_m generates state m and a row in the parsing tables *action* and *goto*. The *goto* table simply contains the numbers of the destination states, as for the deterministic LR algorithm, but the *action* table also inherits probabilistic information from the grammar. The following describes how the actions enter the tables; multiple entries will be needed in cases of ambiguity:

1. For each terminal symbol b, if there are items in I_m such that the total $p_b > \epsilon$, and the shift state n is given by goto$(I_m, b) = I_n$, then

STATE	ACTION							GOTO			
	pn	det	n	pron	iv	tv	$	S	NP	REL	VP
0	sr2	s1						s2	s3		
	0.4	0.6									
1				s4							
				1.0							
2							acc				
							1.0				
3					sr6	s5					sr1
					0.5	0.5					
4			s6		r4	r4	r4			sr3	
			0.3		←	0.7	→				
5	sr2	s1							sr7		
	0.4	0.6									
6					sr6	s5					sr5
					0.5	0.5					

Figure 8.2. SLR and LALR parsing tables for the grammer in Figure 8.1.

$$action[m, b] = \langle \text{shift-to-}n, p_b \rangle$$

2. For each nonterminal symbol B, if $p_B > \epsilon$ and $goto(I_m, B) = I_n$ then
$$goto[m, B] = n$$

3. If $\langle S' \rightarrow S\cdot, p \rangle \in I_m$ then
$$action[m, \$] = \langle \text{accept}, p \rangle$$

4. If $\langle B \rightarrow \gamma\cdot, p \rangle \in I_m$ where $B \neq S'$ then
$$action[m, \text{FOLLOW}(B)] = \langle \text{reduce-by } B \rightarrow \gamma, p \rangle$$

For the very simple grammar shown in Figure 8.1 the parsing tables turn out as shown in Figure 8.2, with shift-reduce optimisation [6,7] applied. The probability of each entry is underneath.

The range of terminal symbols which can follow a B-reduction is given by the set FOLLOW(B) which is obtained from the grammar by the standard algorithm [6]. For a probabilistic grammar, the probability p attached to the reduce item cannot be distributed over those entries because when the tables are compiled it is not determined which of those terminals can actually occur next in that context, so the probability p is attached to the whole range of entries.

The probability associated with a shift action is the prior probability of that terminal occurring next at that point in the input string (assuming no conflicts). Completing the set of prior probabilities involves following up each reduce action using local copies of the stack until shift actions block all further progress. The reduce action probability must be distributed over the shift terminals which emerge (in general a subset of the FOLLOW set). This is done by allocating this probability to the entries in the *action* table row for the state reached after the reduction, in proportion to the probability of each entry. Some of these entries may be further reduce actions in which case a similar procedure must be followed, and so on. Where there is an action conflict, the prior probability of the terminal symbol is the total of the probabilities arrived at in this way.

8.2.2. Canonical LR Parser

For the canonical LR parser each item possesses a lookahead distribution:

$$\langle A \rightarrow \alpha \cdot \beta, p, \{P(a_i)\}_{i=1,/ldots,|T|}\rangle$$

The closure operation is more complex than for the SLR parser, because of the propagation of lookaheads through the non-kernel items. The items to be added to a kernel set to close it take the form

$$\langle B \rightarrow \cdot \gamma_r, p_B p_r, \{P_B(a_j)\}_{j=1,\ldots,|T|}\rangle$$

where $\{P_B(a_j)\}_{i=1,/ldots,|T|}$ is a new lookahead distribution for B. To compute this, suppose that all the items in the closed set with B after the dot are

$$\langle A_k \rightarrow \alpha_k \cdot B\beta_k, p_k, \{P_k(a_i)\}_{i=1,\ldots,|T|}\rangle \text{ for } k = 1, \ldots, n_B$$

A particular probability $P_B(a_j)$ can be regarded as the conditional probability of a_j immediately following an expansion of B: $P(a_j|B)$. Summing over the possible rules and lookahead terminals using the total probability formula gives

$$P_B(a_j) = P(a_j|B) = \sum_{k=1}^{n_B} \sum_{i=1}^{|T|} P(a_j|B, \beta_k, a_i)P(\beta_k, a_i|B)$$

But

$$P(a_j|B, \beta_k, a_i) = P(a_j|\beta_k, a_i)$$

because β_k presupposes the presence of B, and this is the probability of a_j occurring first in a terminal string derived from $\beta_k a_i$, which can be written as $P^F(\beta_k a_i, a_j)$ and is easily evaluated. Also,

$$P(\beta_k, a_i|B) = P(a_i|B, \beta_k)P(\beta_k|B) = P_k(a_i)\frac{p_k}{p_B}$$

because $P(a_i|B, \beta_k)$ is the lookahead probability of a_i for this item, and $P(\beta_k|B)$ is the relative contribution of this item to the total probability of B.

The lookahead distribution for B is therefore given by

$$P_B(a_j) = \sum_{k=1}^{n_B} \frac{p_k}{p_B} \sum_{i=1}^{|T|} P^F(\beta_k a_i, a_j)P_k(a_i)$$

for $j = 1, \ldots, |T|$.

The lookahead distribution is copied to the new kernel set by the goto function. The criterion for testing whether a new set goto(I, X) is already in the collection has an additional component: for each item, the lookahead probability for each terminal must differ from that for its counterpart by at most ϵ.

STATE	ACTION							GOTO			
	pn	det	n	pron	iv	tv	$	S	NP	REL	VP
0	sr2	s1						s2	s3		
	0.4	0.6									
1				s4							
				1.0							
2							acc				
							1.0				
3					sr6	s5					sr1
					0.5	0.5					
4				s6	r4	r4				sr3	
				0.3	0.35	0.35					
5	sr2	s7								sr7	
	0.4	0.6									
6					sr6	s8					sr5
					0.5	0.5					
7			s9								
			1.0								
8	sr2	s1								sr7	
	0.4	0.6									
9				s10		r4				sr3	
				0.3		0.7					
10					sr6	s5					sr5
					0.5	0.5					

Figure 8.3. Canonical parsing tables for the grammer in Figure 8.1.

The first three steps of parsing table construction are essentially the same as for the SLR parser. In step (4), the item in I_m takes the form

$$\langle B \rightarrow \gamma\cdot, p, \{P(a_i)\}_{i=1,\ldots,|T|}\rangle \qquad \text{where } B \neq S'$$

The total probability p has to be distributed over the possible next input symbols a_i, using the lookahead distribution:

$$action[m, a_i] = \langle \text{reduce} - \text{by } B \rightarrow \gamma, pP(a_i)\rangle$$

for all i such that $pP(a_i) > \epsilon$. The prior probabilities during parsing action can now be read directly from the action table.

The canonical parsing tables for the grammar in Figure 8.1 can be seen in Figure 8.3.

8.2.3. LALR Parser

Merging the states of the canonical parser which differ only in lookaheads for each item causes the probability distribution of lookaheads to be lost, so for the

LALR parser the LR(1) items take the form

$$\langle A \to \alpha \cdot \beta, p, L \rangle \qquad \text{where } L \subseteq T.$$

The preferred method for generating the states as described in [6] can be adapted to the probabilistic case. Reduce entries in the parsing tables are then controlled by the lookahead sets, with the prior probabilities found as for the SLR parser. For the simple grammar shown in Figure 8.1 the LALR tables are identical to those for the SLR parser, Figure 8.2.

8.2.4. Interpretation

It is possible to give a Bayesian interpretation for the probabilistic aspects of the algorithm. The discussion which follows, together with that in Section 8.3.1, will use the term "partial parse" to mean a path through (or branch of) the tree of possible interpretations of the input up to a certain point. The word count at any time is denoted by a superscript.

Let $\Gamma_s^{m-1}(s = 1, 2, \ldots)$ represent partial parses up to stage $m - 1$ with a probability for each one given by

$$P(\Gamma_s^{m-1}|\{a\}^{m-1})$$

where $\{a\}^{m-1}$ represents the terminal string $a^1, \ldots, a^{m-1}$. For all versions of the parser this allows for past action conflicts. For the SLR and LALR parsers the set of branches is enlarged by following up any reduce actions in parallel as described in Section 8.2.1. In any case, each branch may contribute to the prediction of terminal a_j^m via a number of items in the corresponding state set:

$$P(a_j^m|\Gamma_s^{m-1}) = \sum_k P(A_k \to \alpha_k \cdot a_j^m \beta_k|\Gamma_s^{m-1})$$

(this calculation is performed when the action table is constructed). The total prior probability of a_j^m is then

$$P(a_j^m|\{a\}^{m-1}) = \sum_s P(a_j^m|\Gamma_j^{m-1})P(\Gamma_s^{m-1}|\{a\}^{m-1}) \qquad (8.1)$$

If the extended branch Γ_s^m is defined as $\Gamma_s^{m-1} \& a_j^m$ then the posterior probability of this if a_j^m is actually observed is

$$P(\Gamma_{s,j}^m|\{a\}^m) = \frac{P(a_j^m|\Gamma_s^{m-1})P(\Gamma_s^{m-1}|\{a\}^{m-1})}{P(a_j^m|\{a\}^{m-1})} \qquad (8.2)$$

where $\{a\}^m$ represents $\{a\}^{m-1}$ extended by a_j^m. For the SLR and LALR parsers all branches predicting anything other than a_j^m fall away, although more than one may still remain because of action conflicts. For each of the LR parsers the computation of (8.1) and (8.2) must be performed during parsing action.

The posterior probability of each item predicting a_j^m is

$$P(A_k \rightarrow \alpha_k a_j^m \cdot \beta_k | \Gamma_{s,j}^m) = \frac{P(a_j^m | A_k \rightarrow \alpha_k \cdot a_j^m \beta_k) P(A_k \rightarrow \alpha_k \cdot a_j^m \beta_k | \Gamma_s^{m-1})}{P(a_j^m | \Gamma_s^{m-1})}$$

$$= \frac{P(A_k \rightarrow \alpha_k \cdot a_j^m \beta_k | \Gamma_s^{m-1})}{P(a_j^m | \Gamma_s^{m-1})}$$

because $P(a_j^m | A_k \rightarrow \alpha_k \cdot a_j^m \beta_k) = 1$. This calculation is embedded into the parsing table generation through the goto function which normalises the probabilities with respect to the total in this way. More generally this applies to

$$P(A_k \rightarrow \alpha_k X \cdot \beta_k | \Gamma_s^{m-1}, X) = \frac{P(A_k \rightarrow \alpha_k \cdot X \beta_k | \Gamma_s^{m-1})}{P(X | \Gamma_s^{m-1})}$$

for any $X \in (N \cup T)$, because if X is a nonterminal then inference of X (by reduction through an X-rule) causes a state transition in essentially the same way as observation of a terminal, and this is how the probabilities are allocated to kernel items as the states are generated. Please note the remarks in Section 8.2.1 about left-recursion with regard to the interpretation of this step.

The manner in which the probabilities are handled during parser generation is therefore intended to support this Bayesian interpretation. Equations (8.1) and (8.2) allow both for action conflicts and (in the case of SLR and LALR parsers) for following up the reduce actions in order to find the prior probabilities, all of which must be done during parsing action.

8.3. Uncertain Input Data

8.3.1. Prediction and Updating Algorithm

We now turn to the action of the parser in the presence of uncertain input data. In keeping with the Bayesian interpretation just advanced, the data are assumed to consist of likelihoods of words. Where this is not the case the method should still apply provided the data consist of relative numerical measures of support for each word.

Let $\Gamma_s^{m-1}(s = 1, 2, \ldots)$ represent partial parses up to stage $m - 1$ as in Section 8.2.4. Let D^m represent the data at stage m, so that $P(D^m | a_j^m)$ is the likelihood of a_j^m, and $\{D\}^m$ represents all the data up to stage m. Each branch Γ_s^{m-1} predicts words a_j^m (perhaps via the LR parser) with probability $P(a_j^m | \Gamma_s^{m-1})$, so the total prior probability for each word a_j^m is

$$P(a_j^m | \{D\}^{m-1}) = \sum_s P(a_j^m | \Gamma_s^{m-1}) P(\Gamma_s^{m-1} | \{D\}^{m-1})$$

Using Bayes' theorem the posterior probabilities of the words are

$$P(a_j^m | \{D\}^m) = \frac{P(D^m | a_j^m) P(a_j^m | \{D\}^{m-1})}{\sum_i P(D^m | a_i^m) P(a_i^m | \{D\}^{m-1})}$$

TERMINAL	STAGE (m)							
	1	2	3	4	5	6	7	8
pn	0.9			0.3	0.4		0.9	
det	0.2		0.4					
n		0.2		0.5				
pron			0.8		0.7			
iv								
tv		0.8	0.1	0.9		0.8		
$								1.0

Figure 8.4. Likelihoods for illustration of uncertainty algorithm.

If we define the extended branch $\Gamma_{s,j}^m$ as $\Gamma_s^{m-1} \& a_j^m$ then after some straightforward manipulation the probability of this is

$$P(\Gamma_{s,j}^m | \{D\}^m) = \frac{P(a_j^m | \Gamma_s^{m-1})P(\Gamma_s^{m-1} | \{D\}^{m-1})}{P(a_j^m | \{D\}^{m-1})} P(a_j^m | \{D\}^m) \quad (8.3)$$

This shows that the posterior probability of a_j^m is distributed over the extended partial parses in proportion to their root parses's contribution to the total prior probability of that word. It also explains the recursive computation mentioned in the Introduction. Branches with small probability $P(\Gamma_{s,j}^m | \{D\}^m) < \epsilon)$ are pruned away, the next set of prior probabilities can be derived and the cycle continues.

These results are derived using the following independence assumptions:

$$P(a_i^k | a_j^m, D^m) = P(a_i^k | a_j^m) \quad \text{and}$$
$$P(D^m | a_j^m, D^k) = P(D^m | a_j^m)$$

which decouple the data at different stages.

Figure 8.4 shows successive likelihoods, entered by hand for a (rather contrived) illustration using the grammar in Figure 8.1. At the end the two viable sentences (with probabilities) are

"pn tv det n pron tv pn" (0.897)
"det n pron tv pn tv pn" (0.103)

Notice that the string which maximises the likelihood at each stage,

"pn tv pron tv pron tv pn"

might correspond to a line of poetry but is not a sentence in the language.

8.3.2. Implementation

The graph-structured stack algorithm of Tomita [1,2] is used for non- deterministic input. The stack graph is split for every possible next word (with nontrivial prior probability) as well as whenever a multiple entry is encountered. Clearly the number of parses grows exponentially with the length of the input string but the probability measure allows all the less- probable ones to be pruned away. Even so the algorithm as currently implemented is computationally more severe than the non-probabilistic Tomita algorithm, for which sub-tree sharing and local ambiguity packing allow an efficient representation of the parse forest. This representation is also used for the probabilistic parser but the individual parse probabilities are stored separately, so that the algorithm in Section 8.3.1 can operate, and to provide a criterion for pruning. The relationship between the stack graph and the parse probabilities implies that splitting the graph requires the entire depth of the graph to be searched, and the implication of this is that the current algorithm requires exponential time. However, devolution of the parse probabilities down through the packed shared forest, together with a suitable revision of the prediction and updating algorithm, should overcome this problem and this refinement is under development.

8.4. Two Complexity Issues

8.4.1. Number of states

The number of states generated for the LR algorithm can be exponential in the size of the grammar, although statistical evidence [8] suggests that in practice it tends to be linear, at least for grammars of computer languages. The introduction of probabilities can result in a real increase in the number of states, as for example in the following probabilistic grammar (similar to one discovered by Lafferty [9]):

$$S \rightarrow a\ A,\ p_1\ |\ b\ A,\ p_2\ |\ a\ B,\ p_3\ |\ b\ B,\ p_4$$
$$A \rightarrow c,\ 1$$
$$B \rightarrow c,\ 1$$

The LALR generator leads to two item sets containing the items

$$\langle A \rightarrow c\cdot,\ p_1/(p_1 + p_3),\ \{\$\}\rangle,\ \langle B \rightarrow c\cdot,\ p_3/(p_1 + p_3),\ \{\$\}\rangle$$

and

$$\langle A \rightarrow c\cdot,\ p_2/(p_2 + p_4),\ \{\$\}\rangle,\ \langle B \rightarrow c\cdot,\ p_4/(p_2 + p_4),\ \{\$\}\rangle$$

respectively, causing a reduce-reduce conflict in each case. These sets are distinguished only by the item probabilities, and an extra state is created. Whether this can lead to a substantial increase in the number of states for the LALR parser is not yet known, but this can certainly happen for the canonical parser. Here we also have the possibility of sets being distinguished only by the lookahead distribution. The simple grammar

$$S \rightarrow S\ S,\ 0.5\ |\ a,\ 0.5$$

causes (theoretically) an infinite sequence of sets to be generated, each containing the reduce item

$$\langle S \rightarrow S \ S \cdot, \ 0.5, \ \{P(a), P(\$)\}\rangle$$

but with a gradually changing lookahead distribution $\{P(a), P(\$)\}$. This occurs because the first rule is both right- and left-recursive. The right-recursion propagates the $ lookahead from set to set and the left-recursion halves it. Clearly this particular problem is rare, and it cannot arise for the SLR and LALR parsers.

8.4.2. *Entropy of the Partial Parses*

Despite the pruning the growth in the number of partial parses, caused both by action conflicts and by the input uncertainty, imposes a serious space and time requirement. Also at the end of the input the number of viable alternatives is a measure of the remaining uncertainty about the input string. However, because the parse probabilities are so variable it is sensible to base the measure of uncertainty upon the entropy of the distribution, rather than simply the number of alternatives.

The "sentence entropy" $\mathcal{H}_S^m$ is defined as the entropy of the partial parses:

$$\mathcal{H}_S^m = -\sum_{s,j} P(\Gamma_{s,j}^m | \{D\}^m) \ln P(\Gamma_{s,j}^m | \{D\}^m)$$

where natural logarithms are used. A related measure called "perplexity" [10], defined as

$$\mathcal{P}_S^m = \exp(\mathcal{H}_S^m)$$

is the equivalent (in entropy) number of equally-likely sentences. Substituting for $P(\Gamma_{s,j}^m | \{D\}^m)$ from equation (8.3) leads to

$$\mathcal{H}_S^m = -\sum_j P(a_j^m | \{D\}^m) \left[\ln P(a_j^m | \{D\}^m) - h_j^m\right]$$

where

$$h_j^m = -\sum_s P(\Gamma_s^{m-1} | a_j^m, \{D\}^{m-1}) \ln P(\Gamma_s^{m-1} | a_j^m, \{D\}^{m-1})$$

is the entropy contributed by the parses at stage $m-1$ predicting word a_j^m. The quantities h_j^m can be evaluated with the prior probabilities.

It can be shown that the sentence entropy has an upper bound as a function of the likelihoods:

$$\mathcal{H}_S^m \leq \ln \sum_j \exp(h_j^m)$$

with equality when

$$P(D^m | a_j^m) \propto \frac{\exp(h_j^m)}{P(a_j^m | \{D\}^{m-1}}.$$

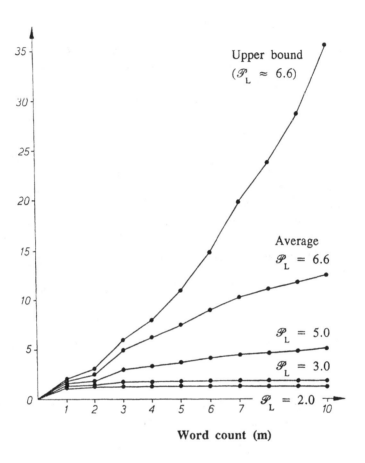

Figure 8.5. Sentence perplexities for grammer ($\mathcal{P}_S$).

The constant of proportionality does not matter. Figure 8.5 shows this upper bound for the grammar in Figure 8.1, and it can be seen that the perplexity is equivalent to 35 equally-likely sentences after 10 words.

The upper bound is very pessimistic because it ignores the discriminative power of the pattern matcher. This could be measured in various ways but it is convenient to define a "likelihood entropy" $\mathcal{H}_L^m$ as

$$\mathcal{H}_L^m = -\sum_j \frac{P(D^m|a_j^m)}{\sum_i P(D^m|a_i^m)} \ln \frac{P(D^m|a_j^m)}{\sum_i P(D^m|a_i^m)}$$

and the "likelihood perplexity" is then $\mathcal{P}_L^m = \exp(\mathcal{H}_L^m)$.

The maximum sentence entropy subject to a fixed likelihood entropy can be found by simulation. Sets of random likelihoods with a given entropy can be generated from sets of independent uniform random numbers by raising these to an appropriate power. The likelihoods are permuted in order to maximise the sentence entropy, fed into the parser and the procedure repeated to simulate the recognition process. The sentence entropy is maximised over a number of such runs.

The likelihoods which produce the upper bound line shown in Figure 8.5 have a perplexity which is approximately constant at 6.6. This line is reproduced almost exactly by the above simulation procedure, using a fixed $\mathcal{P}_L$ of 6.6 with 200 sample runs.

The simulation method is easily adapted to compute the average sentence entropy over the sample runs. For this it is preferable to average the entropy and then convert to a perplexity rather than average the measured perplexity values. This process provides an indication of how the parser will perform in a typical case, assuming a fixed likelihood perplexity as a parameter (although this could be varied from stage to stage if required).

Figure 8.5 shows how the average compares with the maximum for a fixed $\mathcal{P}_L$ of 6.6, and how the sentence perplexity is reduced when the likelihoods are progressively more constrained ($\mathcal{P}_L$ = 5.0, 3.0 and 2.0, for 200 sample runs).

8.4.3. Comparison with Inferred Markov Model

Markov models have some advantages over grammar models for speech recognition (see next section) in flexibility and ease of use but a major disadvantage is their limited memory of past events. For an extended utterance the number of possible sentences compatible with a Markov model may be much greater than for a grammar model, for the same data. Demonstrating this in the present context requires the derivation of a first-order Markov model from a probabilistic grammar [11].

The uncertainty algorithm of Section 8.3.1 will operate largely unchanged with the prior probabilities obtained from the transition probabilities rather than from the LR parser. Figure 8.6 contains results corresponding to those in Figure 8.5, for the first-order Markov model inferred from the grammar in Figure 8.1. The upper bound reaches 409 after 10 words, for a likelihood perplexity of approximately 6.4, reducing to 40 for the average (after 200 sample runs). This falls with the likelihood perplexity but is higher than for the grammar model. The sentence perplexity for the grammar is twice that for the inferred Markov model after from six to ten words depending on $\mathcal{P}_L$. This comparison is reproduced for other grammars considered, including some preliminary work on a grammar developed from an Associated Press corpus for which the average length of sentences is 23 words [12]. For sentences of this length, the uncertainty

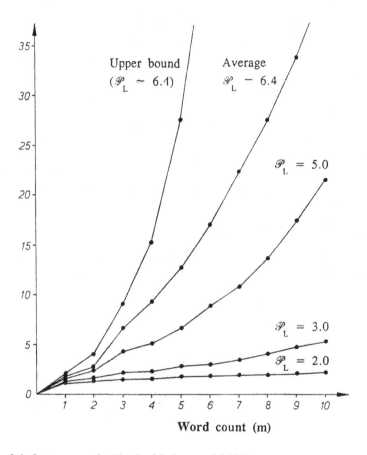

Figure 8.6. Sentence perplexities for Markov model ($\mathcal{P}_S$).

(and space) resulting from the use of a first-order Markov model will greatly exceed that for the grammar model.

8.5. Concluding Remarks

A generalisation of the LR parser to handle probabilistic grammars has been described. The three standard types of LR parser generator (SLR, canonical and LALR) each has a probabilistic extension. The algorithm is capable of treating uncertain input data systematically in conjunction with the probabilistic parsing tables, effectively resulting in an ambiguity superimposed upon that inherent in the grammar and treated using the Tomita graph-structured stack and parse forest packing procedures. Although the current algorithm requires exponential time we anticipate that a polynomial-time version will be forthcoming.

The most immediate application of the probabilistic LR parser is in speech recognition, where at present the spoken words usually have to be separated by deliberate pauses but eventually the demand is for recognition of fluent, connected speech. The degree of difficulty of this task requires recognition to be an active process involving more than signal processing and pattern matching. Models of the language are needed at various levels in order to resolve the many ambiguities and provide the user with a reliable and adaptive system.

Hidden Markov models [13] have proved of great value in modelling word production and hence in pattern matching. Markov models are also often used at the linguistic level [14-16] where they offer great flexibility and computational efficiency. Also being probabilistic they fit naturally into the context of uncertainty created by pattern matching. However, they do not capture the larger-scale structure of language and they do not directly provide an interpretation, merely a transcription of the speech. Grammar models capture more of the structure of language but first the grammars and parsing algorithms need to operate in a context of uncertainty and ambiguity, and second they need to be made at least as adaptable as a Markov model. This chapter has been concerned with the first of these requirements, but the probabilistic LR parser also has a contribution to make to the second, in further work which will be published elsewhere.

It was assumed in Section 8.3 that the pattern matcher returns likelihoods of words, which is true if hidden Markov models are used. Other methods of pattern matching (dynamic time warping, multi-layer perceptrons [17]) return measures which can be treated as likelihoods, and so still fall within the scope of the theory.

The probabilistic LR parser enables a grammar-based model of language to interface with a speech recognition front end as naturally as does a Markov model. The entropy results in section 4 suggest that reliability of speech recognition could be significantly enhanced by the adoption of grammar models, and that this will become even more important when the recognition of fluent, connected speech requires the interpretation of long strings of phonemes.

Acknowledgements

This work was supported by the United Kingdom Science and Engineering Research Council and is now supported by I.B.M. United Kingdom Scientific Centre.

References

[1] Tomita, M., 1986, *Efficient Parsing for Natural Language*", Kluwer Academic Publishers.

[2] Tomita, M., 1990, "Introduction to GLR Parsing," this volume.

[3] Suppes, P., 1968, "Probabilistic Grammars for Natural Languages," *Synthese*, vol 22, pp. 95–116.

[4] Levelt, W. J. M., 1974, *Formal Grammars in Linguistics and Psycholinguistics, volume 1*, Mouton.

[5] Wetherall, C. S., 1980, "Probabilistic Languages: A Review and Some Open Questions," *Computing Surveys*, vol 12, pp. 361–379.

[6] Aho, A. V., Sethi, R., & Ullman, J. D., 1985, *Compilers: Principles, Techniques and Tools*, Addison-Wesley.

[7] Chapman, N. P., 1987, *LR Parsing, Theory and Practice*, Cambridge University Press.

[8] Purdom, P., 1974, "The Size of LALR(1) Parsers," *BIT*, vol 14, pp. 326–337.

[9] Lafferty, J., private communication.

[10] Bahl, L. R., Jelinek, J., & Mercer, R. L., 1983, "A Maximum Likelihood Approach to Continuous Speech Recognition," *IEEE Trans. on Pattern Analysis and Machine Intelligence*, vol PAMI-5, pp. 179–190.

[11] Wright, J. H., 1988, "Linguistic Modelling for Application in Speech Recognition," *Proceedings of the 7th FASE Symposium*, pp. 391–398.

[12] Sharman, R., 1989, "Observational Evidence for a Statistical Model of Language," I.B.M. U.K.S.C. Report 205.

[13] Levinson, S. E., Rabiner, L. R., & Sondhi, M. M., 1983, "An Introduction to the Application of the Theory of Probabilistic Functions of a Markov Process to Automatic Speech Recognition," *BSTJ* vol 62, pp. 1035–1074.

[14] Garside, R., Leech, G., & Sampson, G. (eds), 1987, *The Computational Analysis of English, a Corpus-Based Approach*, Longman.

[15] Jelinek, F., 1985, "The Development of an Experimental Discrete Dictation Recogniser," *Proc IEEE*, vol 73, pp. 1616–1624.

[16] Baker, J. K., 1989, "A Second-Generation Large Vocabulary System," *Speech Technology*, vol 4, pp. 20–24.

[17] Bourland, H. & Wellekens, C. J., 1989, "Speech Pattern Discrimination and Multilayer Perceptrons," *Computer Speech and Language*, vol 3, pp. 1–19.

9   GLR Parsing for Erroneous Input

Stuart Malone and Sue Felshin

9.1. Introduction

The Athena Language Learning Project at MIT is developing advanced educational software for use in the language lab by first through fourth semester foreign language learners. This software must be able to recover from and correct a wide range of morphological, syntactic, and semantic errors, and yet still run in real time. We have developed our system over the course of four years and have used it to write grammars for Spanish, English, French, German, Russian, and Classical Greek; the most comprehensive of these is for Spanish, where the grammar contains over five hundred context-free productions and the lexicon contains some 3000 roots.

This chapter describes the uniform representation for errors used in the parser of the Athena Language Learning Project, which allows the parser to coordinate information from all levels of the system to optimize parsing.

9.2. Terminology

In this chapter, the term *parse* refers to the data structure that represents one possible interpretation of a given input. A GLR parser typically considers many parses simultaneously. We will refer to parses that have reached a final state as *completed parses*.

In order to prioritize parsing, each parse contains an *error count*. The error count of a parse is a measure of the estimated severity of the errors detected so far in that parse. The error count of a parse starts at zero and increases monotonically as parsing proceeds; it may never decrease.

When a specific error is detected, an *error object* (or simply *error*) is created to represent the error and to store any information about the error that the system wishes to maintain. Each error object contains an *error value* that rates the severity of the error. The error count of a parse is simply the sum of the error values of the error objects attached to that parse. Once created, error objects cannot be destroyed.

9.3. Description of the Parser

Conceptually, our parsing system is divided into five levels. *Lexical/morphological analysis* scans the input text, divides it into words, and looks up the words in the lexicon. *Surface filtering* scans these words from left to right, ensuring that linear surface constraints between words are obeyed, and transforming certain constructions into a standardized form for the benefit of the parser. *Structural analysis* is performed by a GLR parsing engine using LALR(1) parsing tables, and builds the the parse trees' hierarchical structure. *Syntactic agreement analysis* performs various kinds of agreement checking between nodes in the parse tree. Finally, *semantic analysis* controls the mapping between syntactic and semantic structure, working from subcategorization frames stored in the lexicon.

In the LALR(1) parsing tables, a Lisp function is associated with each production to perform agreement checking and semantic processing. Most semantic processing takes place at the same time as parsing, not as a separate pass. These Lisp functions may also look directly into the parser stack in order to perform context-sensitive operations like movement and binding.

Given the relaxed rules of our grammars, we did not want the parser to return *every possible* parse of the user's input. A strict grammar for a natural language already has to consider many possible parses of the input – allowing erroneous input increases the problem by an order of magnitude or more. Computing all these parses would be a waste of time, and would make the system unusably slow. Instead, we only want the parser to return the *most likely* parses.

In order to return only the best parses, our parser uses a best-first search strategy with pruning. This pruning is our primary method for reducing the search space and speeding the parsing. Two global parameters control the pruning. The *error limit* specifies how large the error count of a parse may become before that parse is pruned. This parameter provides a limit on how hard the parser will work to interpret its input before giving up. The *style threshold* specifies the range of error counts that the parser should allow, relative to the best completed parse found. For example, if the best completed parse has an error count of 25, then a style threshold of 50 means that all parses with error counts from 25 to 75 should be returned. The style threshold provides a limit to how long the parser will continue to search for other interpretations of the input once the first interpretation has been found.

9.4. Marking Errors

We define objects called *errors* which represent the detection of a language error or other situation which makes the given interpretation of the input unlikely. Each error object contains a numeric value indicating the "severity" of the error.[1]

---

1. Please note the distinction between a grammatical error and an error object. Error objects and error values are used to prioritize parsing, not necessarily to evaluate student error. We may create and attach error objects for situations which are not actually incorrect, but merely unlikely.

Error objects are attached to nodes of the parse tree. Lexical and surface errors are attached to the words (leaves) of the parse tree, while structural, agreement, and semantic errors are attached to the composite nodes of the tree.

For any parse, the total error count of the parse is the sum of the error values of the error objects attached to the nodes in the parse stack and their descendents, plus (in an LALR(1) parser) the error value of the current look-ahead word. This total error count is used to prioritize the parses in the GLR parsing engine, using a best-first search algorithm with pruning.

Since language learners make significantly more syntactic than semantic errors, we perform semantic processing at the same time as syntactic processing. This provides a real advantage, since information from all levels of the system can be used to prioritize and prune the search. This technique saves much time compared to a syntax-only parser, which will generate many parse trees that will be rejected by semantic post-processing. More importantly, with carefully-tuned error values, this method allows the parser to trade off low-level syntactic errors for high-level semantic errors in a uniform and graceful way.

9.5. Types of Errors

We detect errors at each of the five levels within the scope of the parser:

- *lexical/morphological analysis* Errors detected at this level include:
  - *errors in the lexicon* Some errors are so common that we have anticipated them by attaching error objects directly to entries in the lexicon. When lexical lookup encounters one of these errors, the word is automatically marked with the error.
  - *spelling errors* When regular lexical lookup fails, we run a spelling checker to search for known words with similar spellings. Each misspelled word is marked with an error.
  - *blocked word errors* After lexical lookup, a second pass checks to see if the word was "blocked," that is, if a regular form of a word was used where an irregular form should have been used. If so, the word is marked with an error before being returned. For example, the Spanish word "tenió" in place of "tuvo," or the English word "haved" in place of "had."
- *surface filtering* Surface filters look at the stream of words returned by lexical lookup and perform arbitrary surface operations, such as splitting compound words into their components, combining single meanings given by more than one word, and insuring that words are properly contracted. They mark any errors they find on the appropriate words. In English, for instance, a surface filter checks for correct "a/an" alternation as in "a dog" vs. "an apple."
- *structural analysis* The grammar productions anticipate certain structural errors, similar to the way that the lexicon anticipates certain lexical ones. For instance, Spanish detects improper use of preposition-like words, e.g., "encima la mesa" instead of "encima de la mesa" (*"on (top of) the table"*).

Conversely, we may assign a low error value to an error which is quite severe from a pedagogical viewpoint, but which occurs frequently. For instance, failure to use the irregular comparative form of "good" (as in "a gooder book") is a fairly serious error in English, but there is no point in giving it a high error value because it is clear what the student intended.

- *syntactic agreement analysis* The Lisp code associated with each production creates errors as appropriate for any context dependent and/or independent syntactic requirements which are violated by the current constituents. In English, the noun phrase "a books" would be marked with an agreement error and assumed to be plural.
- *semantic analysis* The Lisp code also accesses the case frame interpreter, which builds semantic structure and creates any necessary errors. Even though the semantic structures are separate from the syntactic nodes of the parse tree, semantic errors are marked on the nodes of the parse tree so that they will be visible to the parser.

9.6. An Example

As an example of how this system works, we'll describe the parsing of the sentence "Dije donde llovió," which is incorrect Spanish for *"(I) said where (it) rained."* "Donde" with no accent is a subordinating conjunction, as in "I'll go *where* you go." "Dónde," with an accent, is a pro-PP introducing a complement clause, as in "I said *where* it rained." Unsurprisingly, students of Spanish use the wrong form quite often. Lexical analysis of "donde" in our system returns two words, the subordinating conjunction and the pro-PP, the latter marked with an error value of 500 for the lack of an accent.

The parser starts with a single parse, call it A, where the current word is "dije," the first word in the input sentence. The grammar first pushes various empty nodes onto the parse stack, including an empty COMP and a pro subject, and eventually shifts "dije." Since the next word, "donde," is ambiguous, the parser must now split this parse into two new parses, B and C. Parse B receives the subordinating conjunction as its current word, and has its error count increased by zero. Parse C receives the pro-PP, and has its error count increased by 500. Processing of parse C is then postponed because it's not the best available parse.

Parsing continues with parse B. The subordinate clause "donde llovió" is completed and attached to the S node dominating "dije." Now the sentence is ready to be finished off. But finishing it off precludes the possibility of more arguments being parsed, and the verb "dije," which requires a direct object or complement clause, has received neither. The case frame interpreter creates an error of 600 for a missing argument, and when this is added to parse B, it is no longer the best parse. Thus parse B is now postponed in favor of parse C.

Parsing of C now resumes at the point it was left off, and by parsing "donde llovió" as a complement clause, continues to a successful completion. If the style threshold is less than 100, parsing will stop, and parse C, with an error count of 500, will be returned. Otherwise, parsing of parse B will resume until it is successfully completed with an error count of 600, and both parses B and C will be returned.

9.7. Points of Interest

The above description of our parsing system only provides the general framework within which errors are handled. In our four years of work with this error-handling system, we have developed techniques to handle specific types of errors. These individual error-handling techniques may be implemented independently of each other, but derive their power from their uniform treatment in the GLR parser's best-first search. Here our some of our observations about specific error-handling problems.

9.7.1. Spelling Rules

We use an enhanced version of Karttunen's KIMMO system [1] that is able to both insert and delete multiple characters. However, our KIMMO system is not currently able to create error objects and attach them to the word being scanned, so these errors are misinterpreted as general typographical errors. For instance, if a user of our parsing system types the word "trys" instead of "tries," the system ought to recognize the error as a failure to apply the spelling rule which changes "y+s" to "ies" after a consonant. Conversely, if a user types "plaies" instead of "plays," the system should recognize (probably through a hand-tuned anticipated spelling rule) that the user mistakenly applied the same rule. Slocum [2] describes a system which can handle some of these problems.

We are working on a new system in which we will be able to write spelling rules that create error objects for anticipated spelling errors – much as we currently put entries in the lexicon that contain anticipated errors. In addition to this manual creation of spelling rule errors, the new system will automatically detect and create errors for failure to use an activated spelling rule. Some difficult problems with this system are still being resolved, however.

9.7.2. Handling Typographic Errors

Ideally, the parser should be able to handle typographic errors (typos) the same way that it handles other errors at the lexical level – by simply returning all possible interpretations, both good and bad, and marking the bad interpretations with errors. In practice, however, running a general typo checker on every input word is too slow for an interactive system.[2] Instead, we use a faster, special-purpose checker that only handles capitalization and accent errors, and reserve the slower, general-purpose typo checker for words that cannot otherwise be found in the lexicon.

9.7.3. The Blocker

The language learners who use our system commonly forget about irregular forms of words, and it is important that the system handle these errors gracefully. To do this, we store both regular and irregular forms of words in the lexicon

---

2. at least, given our current computer resources

within the regular stem's entry, and say that the irregular forms "block" their corresponding regular forms. After lexical lookup, a second pass checks the irregular subentries of the returned word to make sure that none of the irregulars blocks the word the student typed. If it determines that one should have, it marks the word with an error before returning it. For example, the regular Spanish word "tenió" is blocked by "tuvo," and the English word "haved" is blocked by "had."

It is necessary to run the blocker to find blocked forms even if there is an unblocked form. For instance, in English the word "seed" could either be the correct singular form of the noun "seed" or the incorrect, blocked past tense of the verb "to see." The parser needs to consider both possibilities so that it will not be stymied when it encounters a sentence like "I seed him."

9.7.4. Anticipated Lexical Errors

Some errors are so common that we have anticipated them by entering them directly into the lexicon. For instance, nouns which take a certain class of endings are also given endings of other classes, marked with errors. Thus we can recognize "abriga" and "abrige" as incorrect attempts to form the Spanish noun "abrigo" (*"overcoat"*). We can also anticipate transference errors; for instance, in Spanish, we anticipate students incorrectly writing "el" (*"the"*) as "le" (French for *"the"*).

Language learners not only use regular forms where they should use irregular ones, but also use irregular forms where they shouldn't. For instance, a Spanish student may use the irregular preterit stem "tuv" to form an imperfect form of "tener", e.g., "tuvía" in place of "tenía." Our blocker does not detect these errors; instead, we must anticipate them in the lexicon by allowing irregular stems to take regular endings, marked with errors.

9.7.5. Input Trees

If all the words in an input string can be identified and are unambiguous, then the data moving from the lexical analyzer to the parser can be repreprepresented simply as a list of words. However, in order to handle ambiguous words, contractions, and surface filters (see Section 9.7.6), a more complicated data structure is needed. We use an *input tree* to represent all of the possible lexical interpretations of the input.[3] For example, the input tree for "He's gone." is represented in Figure 9.1.

With a GLR parser, it is not necessary for all paths through an input tree to have the same length. This allows the lexical analyzer to play games that are not possible using other schemes. For instance, given the incorrect input

---

3. Usually the input tree can be represented more compactly (as it is in our figures) as a directed acyclic graph – but our GLR parser does not make use of this fact.

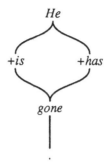

Figure 9.1. A simple input tree.

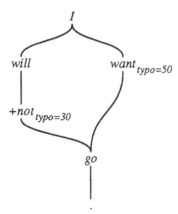

Figure 9.2. An input tree with different length paths.

"I wont go," the recognizer can run the typographic error checker and interpret "wont" either as "won't" or "want," producing the input tree in Figure 9.2.

There is a potential problem with the input tree in Figure 9.2, however. A best-first GLR parser will parse the subject "I" and then proceed down the left branch of the input tree until "+not" becomes the look-ahead token. Since "+not" has an error value of 30, the parser will then back up and try the right branch, only to discover that it contains an even worse error value of 50. The parser will then go back to the parse with an error count of 30, and finish parsing from there. This backtracking is unnecessary, and for longer input, is quite wasteful. The solution is to compute the minimum total error count along all paths of the input tree, and to adjust the error values of the errors in the input tree so that the total error counts of all paths are reduced uniformly by this amount. This guarantees that at least one path through the input tree will have a total error count of zero, and that this unnecessary backtracking won't occur. The resulting tree is in Figure 9.3.

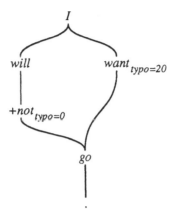

Figure 9.3. An input tree with minimized error values.

9.7.6. Surface Filters

Many linguistic phenomena that occur between words are linear rather than
hierarchical in nature. For instance, the a/an alternation in English is based
entirely on the initial phoneme of the word following a/an, regardless of the
structure containing the two words. In Spanish, the words "de el" ("of the") are
always contracted into "del." Checking these constraints is easier at the linear
level than at the hierarchical level where the words do not necessarily have the
same parent node.

To simplify the handling of these sorts of phenomena we have created a
layer of "surface filters" that separate the GLR parsing engine from the lexical
analyzer. Each surface filter takes an input tree as input and generates a possibly-
modified input tree as output. When a surface filter detects that a surface
constraint has been violated, it can create an error object and attach it to a word
in the input tree.

In our implementation, surface filters also have the ability to insert, delete,
or modify the words themselves, which can be useful for simplifying the
parser's job. For instance, surface filters can expand out all contractions to their
uncontracted forms, so that the parser need only deal with the uncontracted
constructs.

For efficiency's sake, a surface filter should always attach error objects to the
earliest word possible. If a surface filter receives "de el" as input, it should mark
the error for failure to contract on "de" rather than on "el" so that if there is an
entirely different interpretation of the input (say, "de" as a subjunctive form of
"dar," "to give," with a missing accent), it will be tried sooner rather than later.

9.7.7. Anticipated Syntactic Errors

Because the error count of a parse determines whether or not the parse should be actively pursued, postponed, or pruned, it is vitally important for error counts to be accumulated as soon as possible.

Take, for example, the sentence "You drink too much beer." This sentence has two interpretations: the obvious one, and an erroneous one where a case-blocking modifier has been placed between the verb and the direct object (this should read "You drink beer too much."). The error in the second interpretation is in the *placement* of the ADVP "too much" within the VP – there is nothing wrong with the ADVP itself. Conceptually, therefore, the error should be marked on the VP. But before this VP can be built, the erroneous modifier and the direct object must be parsed; this will waste a lot of work before this reading's parse is postponed in favor of the first reading, and eventually pruned unfinished due to the style threshold. Alternatively, we can build a modifier node around the ADVP node and mark the error there, saving the time it takes to parse the direct object. Or best of all, before starting to build the ADVP in the first place, we can build an empty node and mark the error on it. Thus this parse will be postponed as soon as the empty error node is created – before either the ADVP *or* the direct object has been parsed.

We call these errors, which are marked on empty nodes *before* the erroneous input, *anticipated errors*. In many ways, anticipated errors are the most important category of error, because they have the greatest influence on the speed of parsing. Anticipated errors allow us to postpone or prune a parse *before* we have wasted a great deal of time on it.

We handle many structural errors by writing explicit productions to parse ill-formed input, and these errors can always be anticipated. For instance, in our system we can write a rule such as:

```
VP => VBAR MOD,BAD-MOD? OBJ
```

This rule says: "To parse a VP, parse a VBAR, optionally followed by a MOD marked with the BAD-MOD error, followed by an OBJ." This is automatically expanded by our LALR table generator into:

```
VP => VBAR MOD,BAD-MOD? OBJ
MOD,BAD-MOD? =>
MOD,BAD-MOD? => MOD,BAD-MOD
MOD,BAD-MOD => BAD-MOD MOD
BAD-MOD =>                    (create an empty error node)
```

These rules will mark the parse with an error as soon as the parser decides that there is a MOD after the VBAR, *before* the MOD, OBJ, or VP has been created. Since parsing is best first, this parse will be postponed until it is the best parse available – which may never happen. However, if the parse *does* become the best available, the work done to construct the VBAR will not have been wasted. Processing of this parse will continue right where it left off.

This technique of marking errors in the productions also has the advantage that we can target specific structural errors which we expect students of the foreign language to make, including errors caused by transference from the native language, and can simultaneously generate a plausible corrected parse tree. This technique is mentioned briefly by Weischedel and Black [3].

Some structural errors are too complex to anticipate through the use of the LALR table generator's error facility. For example, sbar complement clauses must take different forms depending on the higher verb; compare

```
    I wanted them to leave.
?   I wanted for them to leave.
*   I wanted that they leave.
*   I prayed them to leave.
    I prayed for them to leave.
    I prayed that they leave.
```

Since all three structures ("that" or "for" as the complementizer, or no complementizer at all) are potentially correct, there is no place in any production to create the error.

We can still anticipate the error, however, by having the Lisp code associated with the reducing the complementizer look at the higher verb, which we can find by looking down into the parse stack. We examine the subcategorization frame of this verb to see if it allows an SBAR complement clause, and if so, whether it allows the given complementizer. We create a small error if the wrong complementizer was used and a very large error if no clause is allowed at all.

9.7.8. Semantic Ambiguity

Since we expect language learners to make many more syntactic and morphological errors than semantic errors, our parser performs semantic analysis at the same time as syntactic analysis in order to reduce ambiguity early. One syntactic interpretation of a sentence may, of course, have many semantic interpretations; compare

```
    I painted the wall with a brush.
    I painted the wall with a vengeance.
    I painted the wall with Mary.
```

By packing ambiguous semantic information into a single parse, we avoid having to create separate parses for each semantic interpretation of a given syntactic structure. But the error count of the semantic interpretation of a phrase has to be included in the error count of the parse which contains it, so that it may be used for prioritizing parsing. Since error objects may only be created, and the error count of a parse may only increase, we may safely define the semantic error count of a phrase as the error count of its best semantic interpretation. Whenever we add information to the semantic interpretation of a phrase, the error count of the parse containing it increases by the difference between the error counts of the old and new best semantic interpretations.

Because semantic interpretations of a phrase can become highly ambiguous (a "with" phrase can usually be interpreted at least three ways), we can save time by postponing semantic processing whenever possible. All we need is the error count of the *best* interpretation; once we have found it we can postpone processing of all other interpretations. When parsing is completed, we need complete semantic processing for only the successful parses.

9.8. Concluding Remarks

In our work at the Athena Language Learning Project, we have created a framework in which errors at all levels of parsing can be integrated and considered together. Using this framework, we have built grammars which can parse well-formed sentences of low to moderate complexity and ill-formed sentences of low complexity in real time (less than 10 seconds). Sentences can contain errors in spelling, morphology, syntactic structure and agreement, and semantic usage, and yet still be interpreted "correctly" by the system. Even ill-formed sentences must be highly ambiguous before parsing slows to more than a couple of minutes. With a wide coverage of ill-formed input, we have found that ambiguous clause boundaries remain the primary cause of slow parsing.

We plan improvements to our morphological processor and typographical error checker. Further research is also necessary on methods of automatically tuning error values, presumably using a large corpus of well- and ill-formed input.

Acknowledgement

We wish to thank the Athena Language Learning Project's director, Dr. Janet H. Murray, and technical advisor, Professor Robert C. Berwick, for supporting our research and encouraging us to write about our work.

References

[1] Karttunen, L., 1983, "KIMMO: A General Morphological Processor," in *Texas Linguistic Forum 22*, pp. 165–186.

[2] Slocum, J., 1988, "Morphological Processing in the Nabu System," in *Second Conference on Applied Natural Language Processing*, pp. 228–234.

[3] Weischedel, R. M. & Black, J. E., 1980 (April-June), "Responding Intelligently to Unparsable Inputs," *American Journal of Computation Linguistics*, 6(2):97–109.

10 GLR Parsing for Noisy Input

Hiroaki Saito and Masaru Tomita

10.1. Introduction

There have been a few attempts to integrate a speech recognition device with a natural language understanding system. Hayes *et. al* [5] adopted the technique of *caseframe instantiation* to parse a continuously spoken English sentence in the form of a *word lattice* (a set of word candidates hypothesized by a speech recognition module) and produce a frame representation of the utterance. Poesio and Rullent [4] suggested a modified implementation of the caseframe parsing to parse a word lattice in Italian. Lee *et. al* [1] developed a prototype Chinese (Mandarin) dictation machine which takes a syllable lattice (a set of syllables, such as [guo-2] and [tieng-1], hypothesized by a speech recognition module) and produces a Chinese character sequence which is both syntactically and semantically sound.

In this chapter, we try to parse a Japanese utterance in the form of a sequence of phonemes.[1] Our speech recognition device, which is a high-speed speaker-independent system developed by Matsushita Research Institute [2,3], takes a continuous speech utterance, for example "megaitai" ("I have a pain in my eye"), from a microphone and produces a *noisy* phoneme sequence such as "ebaitaai."[2]

The speech recognition device does not have any syntactic or semantic knowledge. More input/output examples of the speech device are presented below:

<Correct sequence of phonemes>		*<Recognition output>*
igamukamukasuru	→	igagukamukusjuru
kubigakowabaqteiru	→	kubigakooboqteiiru
atamagaitai	→	otomogaitai

Note that the speech recognition device produces a phoneme sequence, not a phoneme lattice; there are no other phoneme candidates available as alternates. We must make the best guess based solely on the phoneme sequence generated by the speech device. Errors caused by the speech device can be classified into three groups:

- *Substituted Phonemes* – Phonemes recognized incorrectly. The second phoneme /b/ in "ebaitaai" is a substituted phoneme, for example.

---

1. Phonemes (e.g. /g/, /a/, /s/, etc.) are even lower level units than syllables.
2. We distinguish *noisy* from *ill-formed*. The former is due to recognition device errors, while the latter is due to human users.

- *Deleted Phonemes* – Phonemes which are actually spoken but not recognized by the device. For example a phoneme /m/ is missed at the beginning of "ebaitaai."
- *Inserted Phonemes* – Phonemes recognized by the device which are not actually spoken. The penultimate phoneme /a/ in "ebaitaai," for example, is an inserted phoneme.

To cope with these problems, we need:

1. A very efficient parsing algorithm, as our task requires much more search than conventional typed sentence parsing. And
2. A good scoring scheme, to select the most likely sentence out of multiple candidates.

In Sections 10.2 and 10.3, we describe the parsing algorithm and the scoring scheme, respectively.

10.2. The Parsing Algorithm

The grammar we are using is an Augmented Context-Free Grammar whose terminal symbols are phonemes rather than words. That is, the grammar includes rules like

    Noun → w a t a s i

instead of

    Noun → 'watasi.'

Therefore parsing proceeds character by character (phoneme by phoneme). The grammar has been developed primarily for CMU's knowledge-based machine translation system [9], and consists of more than 2000 rules including lexical rules like one above.[3]

10.2.1. Generalized LR Parsing

Tomita [7,10] introduced the *Generalized LR Parsing Algorithm* for Augmented Context-Free Grammars, which can ingeniously handle nondeterminism and ambiguity with a *graph-structured stack*. Tomita also showed that it can be used for a word lattice parsing [8]. Our algorithm here is based on Tomita's parsing algorithm.

A very simple example grammar is shown in Figure 10.1, and its LR parsing table, compiled automatically from the grammar, is shown in Figure 10.2.

Grammar symbols of lower case characters are terminals. Entries "s *n*" in the action table (the left part of the table) indicate the action "shift one word from input buffer onto the stack and go to state *n*." Entries "r *n*" indicate the action "reduce constituents on the stack using rule *n*." The entry "acc" stands for the action "accept," and blank spaces represent "error." The goto table (the right part of the table) decides to which state the parser should go after a

---

3. The run-time grammar, which contains both syntax and semantics, is compiled automatically from more abstract formalisms: the Functional Grammar Formalism for syntax and frame representation for semantics. More discussions on this *Universal Parser Architecture* are described in [9].

(1)	S	→	NP PD
(2)	S	→	N
(3)	S	→	PD
(4)	NP	→	N P
(5)	N	→	m e
(6)	N	→	i
(7)	P	→	g a
(8)	PD	→	i t a i

Figure 10.1. An example grammar.

State	*	a	i	e	m	g	t	\$	N	NP	P	PD	S
									|				
0			s4		s5				2	3		1	6
1	r3												
2	r2					s7					8		
3			s9									10	
4	r6						s11						
5				s12									
6								acc					
7		s13											
8	r4												
9						s11							
10	r1												
11		s14											
12	r5												
13	r7												
14			s15										
15	r8												

The *Action Table* spans columns *, a, i, e, m, g, t, \$. The *Goto Table* spans columns N, NP, P, PD, S.

Figure 10.2. LR parsing table.

reduce action. In case there are multiple actions in one entry, it executes all the actions with the graph-structured stack. Terminal symbol "*" in the action table is a wild card character with which the state is ready for the reduce action. (Figure 10.2 is an LR(0) parsing table.)

10.2.2. Handling Substituted, Inserted, and Deleted Phonemes

To cope with substituted, inserted and deleted phonemes, the parser must consider these errors as it parses an input from left to right. While the algorithm described in the previous subsection cannot handle these noisy phenomena, it is well suited to consider many possibilities at the same time, and therefore, it can be relatively easily modified to handle such noisy phenomena as the following.

- *Substituted phonemes*
  Each phoneme in a phoneme sequence may have been substituted and thus may be incorrect. The parser has to consider all these possibilities. We can create a phoneme lattice dynamically by placing alternate phoneme candidates in the same location as

| 1 | 2 | 3 | 4 | 5 | 6 | 7 | 8 | 9 | 10 | 11 | 12 | 13 | 14 | 15 | 16 | 17 |
| | e | | b | | a | | i | | t | | a | | a | | i | |

Figure 10.3. An input sequence of phonemes.

the original phoneme. Each possibility is then explored by each branch of the parser. Not all phonemes can be substituted to any other phoneme. For example, while /o/ can be mis-recognized as /u/, /i/ can never be mis-recognized as /o/. This kind of information can be obtained from a *confusion matrix*, which we shall discuss in the next section. With the confusion matrix, the parser does not have to exhaustively create alternate phoneme candidates.

- *Inserted phonemes*
  Each phoneme in a phoneme sequence may be an extra, and the parser has to consider these possibilities. We have one branch of the parser consider an inserted phoneme by simply ignoring the phoneme. The parser assumes at most one inserted phoneme can exist between two real phonemes.
- *Deleted phonemes*
  Deleted phonemes can be handled by inserting possible deleted phonemes between two real phonemes. The parser assumes that at most one phoneme can be missing between two real phonemes, and we have found the assumption quite reasonable and safe.

10.2.3. An Example

In this subsection, we present a sample trace of the parser. Here we use the grammar in Figure 10.1 and the LR table in Figure 10.2 to try to parse the phoneme sequence "ebaitaai" represented in Figure 10.3. The right sequence is "megaitai" which means "I have a pain in my eye."

In this example we make the following assumptions for substituted and deleted phonemes.

- /i/ may possibly be mis-recognized as /e/.
- /e/ may possibly be mis-recognized as /a/.
- /g/ may possibly be mis-recognized as /b/.
- /m/ may be missed in the output sequence with a higher probability.

Now we begin parsing: first an initial state 0 is created. The action table indicates that the initial state is expecting "m" and "i" (Figure 10.4a). Since the parsing proceeds strictly from left to right, the parser looks for the deleted phoneme candidates between the first time frame 1 − 2. (We will use the term T1, T2, ... for representing the time1, time2, ... in Figure 10.3.) Only the deleted phoneme "m" in this group is applicable to state 0. The new state number 5 is determined from the action table (Figure 10.4b).

The next group of phonemes between T2 and T3 consists of the "e" phoneme in the phoneme sequence and the substituted candidate phonemes of "e." In this group "e" is expected by state 5 and "i" is expected by state 0 (Figure 10.4c). After "e" is taken, the new state is 12, which is ready for the action "reduce 5." Thus, using the rule 5 (N → m e), we reduce the phonemes "m e" into N. From state 0 with the nonterminal N, state 2 is determined from the goto

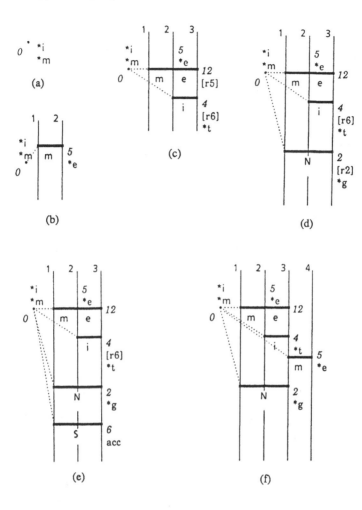

Figure 10.4. Parsing action table for input sequence in Figure 10.3.

table. The action table, then, indicates that state 2 has a multiple entry, i.e., state 2 is expecting "g" and ready for the reduce action (Figure 10.4d). Thus, we reduce the nonterminal N into S by rule 2 (S → N), and the new number 6 is determined from the goto table (Figure 10.4e). The action table indicates that state 6 is an accept state, which means that "m e" is a successful parse. But only the first phoneme "e" of the input sequence "ebaitaai" is consumed at this point. Thus we discard this parse by the following constraint.

[**Constraint 1**] The successful parse should consume the phonemes at least until the phoneme just before the end of the input sequence.

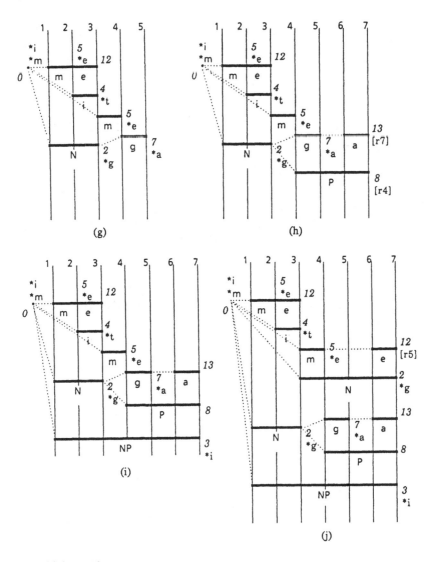

Figure 10.4. contd.

Note that only the parse S in Figure 10.4e is ignored and that the nonterminal N in Figure 10.4d is alive.

Now we return to the Figure 10.4c and continue the shift action of "i." After "i" is taken, the new state 4 is determined from the action table. This state has a multiple entry, i.e. state 4 is expecting "t" and ready for the reduce action. Thus we reduce "i" into N by rule 6. Here we use the *local ambiguity packing*

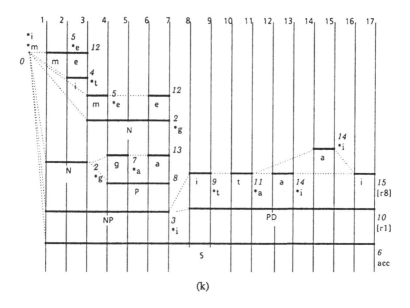

(k)

Figure 10.4. contd.

technique, because the reduced nonterminal is the same, the starting state is 0 for both, and the new state is 2 for both. Thus we do not create the new nonterminal N.

Now we go on to the next group of phonemes between T3 and T4. Only "m" is applied to the initial state (Figure 10.4f).

The next group of phonemes between T4 and T5 has one applicable phoneme, i.e. a substituted phoneme candidate "g" to state 2. After "g" is taken, the new state 7 is determined from the action table (Figure 10.g). The next group of phonemes between T5 and T6 has only one applicable phoneme; a deleted phoneme candidate "m" to state 0. Here we can introduce another constraint which discards this partial-parse.

[**Constraint 2**] After consuming two phonemes of the input sequence, no phonemes can be applied to the initial state 0.

This constraint is natural because it is unlikely that more than two phonemes are recorded before the actual beginning phoneme for our speech recognition device.

The next group of phonemes between T6 and T7 has two applicable phonemes, i.e. the output phoneme "a" to state 7 and the substituted phoneme candidate "e" to state 5. After "a" is taken, the new state 7 is ready for the reduce action. Thus, we reduce "g a" into P by rule 7 (Figure 10.4h). The new state 8 is determined by the goto table, and is also ready for the reduce action.

IN OUT	/a/	/o/	/u/	/i/	/e/	/j/	/w/	...	(I)	(II)
/a/	93.8	1.1	1.3	0	2.7	0	0	...	0.9	5477
/o/	2.4	84.3	5.8	0	0.3	0	0.6	...	6.5	7529
/u/	0.3	1.8	79.7	2.4	4.6	0.1	0	...	9.7	5722
/l/	0.2	0	0.9	91.2	3.5	0.7	0	...	2.9	6158
/e/	1.9	0	4.5	3.3	89.1	0.1	0	...	1.1	3248
/j/	0	0	1.1	2.3	2.2	80.1	0.3	...	11.4	2660
/w/	0.2	5.1	5.8	0.5	0	2.6	56.1	...	11.2	428
.	.	.	.	.	.	.	.	.	.	.
.	.	.	.	.	.	.	.	.	.	.
(III)	327	176	564	512	290	864	212	...		

(I)	rate of deleted phonemes
(II)	total number of samples
(III)	number of inserted phonemes

Figure 10.5. A confusion matrix (portion).

Thus we reduce "N P" into NP by rule 4 (Figure 10.4i). The new state is 3. In applying "e," there are two "state 2"s: one is "m" between T1 and T2; the other one is "m" between T3 and T4. Here we can introduce a third constraint which discards the former partial-parse.

[**Constraint 3**] A shift action is not applied when the distance between the phoneme and the applied (non)terminal is more than 3. (This distance contains at least one real phoneme.)

Figure 10.4j shows the situation after "e" is applied.

The parsing continues in this way, and the final situation is shown in Figure 10.4k. As a result, the parser finds two successful parses; "megaitai" and "igaitai (I have a stomachache)."

10.3. Scoring and the Confusion Matrix

There are two main reasons why we want to score each parse: first, to prune the search space by discarding branches of the parse whose score is hopelessly low; second, to select the best sentence out of multiple candidates by comparing their scores.

Branches of the parse which consider fewer substituted/inserted/deleted phonemes should be given higher scores. Whenever a branch of the parse handles a substituted/inserted/deleted phoneme, a specific penalty is given to the branch. Unfortunately, the recognition device does not give us the probability of each phoneme in the sequence nor the substituted/inserted/deleted phoneme information. Namely only the phoneme sequence is given. Therefore we use the confusion matrix for scoring.

Figure 10.5 shows a part of the confusion matrix made by the manufacturer of the recognition device from the large word data. This matrix tells us, for example, that if the phoneme /a/ is inputed, then the device recognizes it correctly 93.8% of the time; mis-recognizes it as /o/ 1.1% of the time, as /u/ 1.3% of the time, and so on. The column (I) says that the input is missed 0.9% of the time.

Conversely, if the phoneme /o/ is generated from the device, there is a slight chance that the original input was /a/, /u/ and /w/, respectively, but no chance that the original input was /i/, /e/ or /j/. The probability of the original input being /a/ is much higher than being /w/. Thus, a substituted phoneme /w/ should be given a more severe penalty than /a/. A score for substituted phonemes can be obtained in this way, deleted phonemes should be given a negative score, and inserted phonemes should be given a zero or a negative score. With this scoring a score of a partial parse is calculated by summing up the score of each constituent. Therefore, the more likely parse has a higher score.

Two method have been adopted to prune partial parses by a score:

- Discarding the low-score shift-waiting branches when a phoneme is applied.
- Discarding the low-score branches in a local ambiguity packing.

The former method is very effective when strictly applied.

The confusion matrix only shows us the phoneme-to-phoneme transition, therefore a broader unit transition should also be considered, such as a tendency for the /w/ phoneme in "owa" or "owo" to be missed or for the very first /h/ sound of an input to be missed, and the frequent transformation to "h@" of the "su" sound in "desuka."

10.4. Concluding Remarks

The parser has been implemented in Common Lisp on a Symbolics Lisp Machine and is being integrated into CMU's knowledge-based machine translation system to accept a spoken Japanese sentence in the domain of doctor-patient conversation and generate sentences in English, German and Japanese.

The parser has been tested against five persons. Each person pronounced 27 sentences in which long sentences are not included due to the limits of the speech recognition device. 84% of the inputs are parsed correctly and the right sentence appears as the best-score candidate in 88% out of the correctly parsed inputs. The average parsing time for one sentence is 82 seconds.

Acknowledgements

The authors would like to thank Shuji Morii for giving us the opportunity to use the speech recognition device and to thank other members of the Center for Machine Translation for useful comments and advices. We are also indebted to ATR Interpreting Telephony Research Laboratories for providing the computational environment.

```
Command: input
"ebaitaai"
Command: (parse-s)
Evaluation of (PARSE) took 30.524798 seconds of elapsed time
including 5.003 seconds waiting for the disk for 8 faults.
The garbage collector has flipped, so consing was not measured.4 parses found

1: (185) M(1-2#-10) E(2-3#30) G(4-5#10) A(6-7#32) I(8-9#30) I(10-11#31) A(12-13#32) I(16-17#30)

((MOOD ((ROOT DEC))) (SEM *HAVE-A-PAIN1002) (OBJ ((:WH -) (CASE GA) (SEM *EYE) (ROOT ME))) (CAUSATIVE -) (OBJ-CASE GA)
 (SUBJ-CASE GA) (SUBCAT 2ARG-GA) (CAT ADJ) (TIME ((ROOT PRESENT))) (ROOT ITAI)))

2: (172) I(2-3#7) G(4-5#10) A(6-7#32) I(8-9#30) T(10-11#31) A(12-13#32) I(16-17#30)

((MOOD ((ROOT DEC))) (SEM *HAVE-A-PAIN010) (OBJ ((:WH -) (CASE GA) (SEM *STOMACH) (ROOT I))) (CAUSATIVE -) (OBJ-CASE GA)
 (SUBJ-CASE GA) (SUBCAT 2ARG-GA) (CAT ADJ) (TIME ((ROOT PRESENT))) (ROOT ITAI)))

3: (115) I(2-3#7) I(4-5#1) A(6-7#32) I(8-9#30) K(10-11#13) A(12-13#32)

((SEM *HAVE-A-PAIN930) (TIME ((ROOT (*OR* PRESENT FUTURE)))) (MOOD ((ROOT QUES))) (OBJ-CASE GA) (SUBJ-CASE GA) (SUBCAT 2ARG-GA)
 (CAT ADJ) (ROOT ITAI))

4: (110) M(4-5#3) A(6-7#32) I(8-9#30) K(10-11#13) A(12-13#32)

((SEM *HAVE-A-FEVER46) (TIME ((ROOT (*OR* PRESENT FUTURE)))) (MOOD ((ROOT QUES))) (OBJ-CASE GA) (SUBJ-CASE GA) (CAUSATIVE -)
 (PASSIVE -) (SUBCAT STAT) (NEGATION ((ROOT HITEI))) (CAT V) (ROOT ARU))

T
Command: ▮
```

```
Command: (evaldata 25 25)
25: "AZUBI#AKOABAQCIIRU"

Evaluation of (PARSE) took 83.099357 seconds of elapsed time
including 13.183 seconds waiting for the disk for 85 faults.
The garbage collector has flipped, so consing was not measured.

2 parses found.

1: (400) K(4-5#4) U(6-7#29) B(8-9#29) I(10-11#30) G(12-13#33) A(14-15#32) K(16-17#32) O(18-19#24) W(19-20#0) A(20-21#16) B(22-23#
29) A(24-25#32) Q(26-27#27) T(28-29#3) E(30-31#2) I(32-33#30) R(34-35#31) U(36-37#29)

((MOOD ((ROOT DEC))) (SEM *HAVE-A-STIFFNESS1260) (OBJ ((:WH -) (CASE GA) (SEM *NECK) (ROOT KUBI))) (CAUSATIVE -) (OBJ-CASE GA)
 (SUBJ-CASE GA) (PASSIVE -) (SUBCAT STAT) (TIME ((ROOT (*OR* PRESENT FUTURE)))) (PROGRESSIVE -) (CAT V) (ROOT KOWABARU))

2: (296) K(4-5#4) U(6-7#29) B(8-9#29) I(10-11#30) G(12-13#33) A(14-15#32) K(16-17#28) O(18-19#24) W(19-20#0) A(20-21#16) B(22-23#
29) A(24-25#32) Q(26-27#27) T(28-29#3) A(29-30#-20)

((MOOD ((ROOT DEC))) (SEM *HAVE-A-STIFFNESS1264) (OBJ ((:WH -) (CASE GA) (SEM *NECK) (ROOT KUBI))) (CAUSATIVE -) (OBJ-CASE GA)
 (SUBJ-CASE GA) (PASSIVE -) (SUBCAT STAT) (TIME ((ROOT PAST))) (CAT V) (ROOT KOWABARU))

=======================
22 too short parses found

1: (202) K(4-5#4) U(6-7#29) B(8-9#29) I(10-11#30) G(12-13#33) A(14-15#32) K(16-17#28) O(18-19#24) R(22-23#3) U(23-24#-10)

((MOOD ((ROOT DEC))) (SEM *HAVE-A-STIFFNESS1260) (OBJ ((:WH -) (CASE GA) (SEM *NECK) (ROOT KUBI))) (CAUSATIVE -) (OBJ-CASE GA)
 (SUBJ-CASE GA) (PASSIVE -) (SUBCAT STAT) (TIME ((ROOT (*OR* PRESENT FUTURE)))) (CAT V) (ROOT KORU))

2: (96) A(2-3#32) C(4-5#5) U(6-7#29) I(10-11#30)

((MOOD ((ROOT DEC))) (SUBJ-CASE GA) (SUBCAT 1ARG) (CAT ADJ) (TIME ((ROOT PRESENT))) (SEM *HOT) (ROOT ATUI))

3: (66) A(2-3#32) A(4-5#2) U(6-7#29) K(8-9#1) U(10-11#2)

((MOOD ((ROOT DEC))) (SUBJ-CASE GA) (CAUSATIVE -) (PASSIVE -) (SUBCAT IHTRANS) (SEM *WALK936)
 (TIME ((ROOT *OR* PRESENT FUTURE)))) (CAT V) (ROOT ARUKU))

4: (63) A(2-3#32) R(4-5#2) U(6-7#29)

((MOOD ((ROOT DEC))) (OBJ-CASE GA) (SUBJ-CASE GA) (CAUSATIVE -) (PASSIVE -) (SUBCAT STAT) (SEM *HAVE-A-FEVER230)
 (TIME ((ROOT *OR* PRESENT FUTURE)))) (CAT V) (ROOT ARU))

5: (55) A(2-3#32) C(4-5#5) U(6-7#29) I(7-8#-11)

((MOOD ((ROOT DEC))) (SUBJ-CASE GA) (SUBCAT 1ARG) (CAT ADJ) (TIME ((ROOT PRESENT))) (SEM *HOT) (ROOT ATUI))

6: (52) H(1-2#0) A(2-3#32) I(3-4#-11) R(4-5#2) U(6-7#29)
**MORE**▮
```

Dynamic Lisp Listener 15

Figure 10.6. Sample runs of parser.

Sample Runs

Two actual outputs of the parser are shown in Figure 10.6. The first input phoneme sequence is "ebaitaai" and the correct sequence is "megaitai" (which is the same sentence as in the example in Section 10.2), which is produced as the top-score sentence of all parses. The second input sequence is "azubi-gakoabaqciiru" and the correct sequence is "kubigakowabaqteiru" (which means

"I have a stiff neck"). The frame-structure output after each parse is the meaning of the sentence. This meaning is extracted in the same way the CMU's machine translation system does. Namely, each rule of the context free grammar has a function which is executed each time the rule is applied (i.e. when the reduce action occurs.). If the function returns nil, this partial parse is discarded because the parse is not correct semantically. If the function returns a non-nil value, the value becomes the semantic of the right-hand-side of the rule and is forwarded to the left-hand-side nonterminal symbol. The details are described in [6].

References

[1] Lee, L. S., Tseng, C. Y., Chen, K. J., and Huang, J. (August 1987), "The preliminary results of a Mandarin dictation machine based upon Chinese natural language analysis," in *Proceedings of the Tenth International Joint Conference on Artificial Intelligence*, Milan.

[2] Morli, S., Niyada, K., Fujii, S., and Hoshimi, M. (March 1985), "Large vocabulary speaker-independent Japanese speech recognition system," in *IEEE International Conference on Acoustics, Speech, and Signal Processing (ICASSP85)*.

[3] Hiraoka, S., Morli, S., Hoshimi, M., and Niyada, K. (April 1986), "Compact isolated word recognition system for large vocabulary," in *IEEE-IECEJ-ASJ International Conference on Acoustics, Speech, and Signal Processing (ICASSP86)*, Tokyo.

[4] Poesio, M., and Rullent, C. (August 1987), "Modified caseframe parsing for speech understanding systems," in *Proceedings of the Tenth International Joint Conference on Artificial Intelligence*, Milan.

[5] Hayes, P. J., Hauptmann, A. G., Carbonell, J. G., and Tomita, M. (August 1986), "Parsing spoken language: A semantic caseframe approach," in *11th International Conference on Computational Linguistics (COLING86)*, Bonn, U.K.

[6] Tomita, M. and Carbonell, J. G. (May 1987), *The universal parser architecture for knowledge-based machine translation*, Technical report CMU-CMT-87-101, Center for Machine Translation, Carnegie Mellon University.

[7] Tomita, M. (1985), *Efficient Parsing for Natural Language: A Fast Algorithm for Practical Systems*, Kluwer Academic Publishers, Boston, MA.

[8] Tomita, M. (April 1986), "An efficient word lattice parsing algorithm for continuous speech recognition," in *IEEE-IECEJ-ASJ International Conference on Acoustics, Speech, and Signal Processing (ICASSP86)*, Tokyo.

[9] Tomita, M. and Carbonell, J. G. (August 1987), "The universal parser architecture for knowledge-based machine translation," in *10th International Joint Conference on Artificial Intelligence (IJCAI87)*.

[10] Tomita, M. (1987), "An efficient augmented-context-free parsing algorithm," *Computational Linguistics*.

11   GLR Parsing in Hidden Markov Model

Kenji Kita, Takeshi Kawabata, and Hiroaki Saito

11.1. Introduction

This chapter describes the application of Generalized LR parsing to speech recognition. In particular, we will focus on a method called *HMM-LR*, first introduced by [5], which is an integration of Hidden Markov Models and Generalized LR parsing.

Speech recognition is a technology that transforms an utterance into a text. With this technology, we can construct an intelligent machine that can listen to a speech utterance and then carry out the instructions appropriately. There have been many approaches to speech recognition, for example:

1. The *Feature-Based* approach [20],
2. The *Neural Network* approach [11,18],
3. The *Hidden Markov Model* approach [3,8].

Among these, the Hidden Markov Model is now the most widely used approach. The Hidden Markov Model is a powerful stochastic model and it has the ability to cope with the acoustical variations of speech. Moreover, any word models can be composed of phone models, thus it is easy to construct a large vocabulary speech recognition system.

One of the major problems in speech recognition is coping with large search spaces. As search space size increases, recognition performance decreases. Grammatical constraints are effective in reducing the search space and hence increase processing speed and recognition accuracy. Generalized LR parsing is one of the best mechanisms for dealing with grammatical constraints based on a context-free grammar.

There are two approaches using natural language parsers. In the first approach, the speech recognizer and the parser are used independently, that is, the speech recognizer is used to produce a phone/word *lattice* (a set of hypothesized phones/words with different starting and ending positions in the input speech). Then the parser is applied to obtain legal phone/word sequences. The second approach is to use grammatical constraints during speech recognition. It goes without saying that the first approach is not desirable, because of the information loss due to signal-symbol conversion. In HMM-LR, the LR parser drives Hidden Markov Models directly without any intervening structures such as a phone/word lattice. Thus, very accurate and efficient speech parsing is achieved.

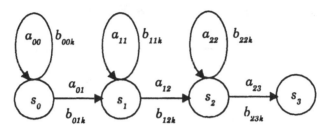

Figure 11.1. An example of a Hidden Markov Model.

11.2. Hidden Markov Models

Hidden Markov Models (HMM) [9,15,16] are effective in expressing speech statistically and have been used widely for speech recognition.

11.2.1. Basic Concepts

An example of a Hidden Markov Model is shown in Figure 11.1. A model has a collection of *states* connected by *transitions*. Two sets of probabilities are attached to each transition. One is a *transition probability* a_{ij}, which provides the probability for taking a transition from state i to state j. The other is an *output probability* $b_{ij}(k)$, which provides the probability of emitting symbol k when taking a transition from state i to state j.

Formally, a Hidden Markov Model M is defined by a 4-tuple $M = (S, Y, A, B)$.

- S : A set of states $\{s_i\}$ including an initial state S_I and a final state S_F.
- Y : A set of output symbols.
- A : A set of transitions $\{a_{ij}\}$ where a_{ij} is the probability of taking a transition from state i to state j, and $\sum_j a_{ij} = 1$.
- B : The output probability distribution $\{b_{ij}(k)\}$ where $b_{ij}(k)$ is the probability of emitting symbol k when taking a transition from state i to state j, and $\sum_k b_{ij}(k) = 1$.

Typically, *vector quantization* (VQ) [10] is used as the acoustic front-end for HMM. Vector quantization is a discrete representation of spectral space. A set of fixed prototype vectors is called a *codebook*, and an output symbol of a model comes from these prototype vectors.

11.2.2. Recognition Problem

In a stochastic approach, having observed acoustic data y, a speech recognizer must decide a word sequence $\hat{w}$ that satisfies the following condition:

$$P(\hat{w}|y) = \max_w P(w|y)$$

By Bayes' rule,

HMM
STATE

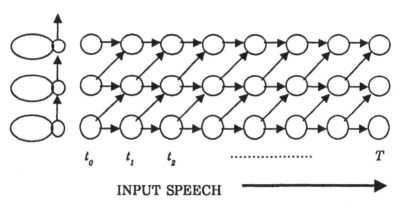

Figure 11.2. A trellis diagram.

$$P(w|y) = \frac{P(y|w)P(w)}{P(y)}$$

Since $P(y)$ does not depend on w, maximizing $P(w|y)$ is equivalent to maximizing $P(y|w)P(w)$. $P(w)$ is the *a priori* probability that the word sequence w will be uttered, and is estimated by the *language model*. In the case of a language model where all words are equally likely, this term is negligible. $P(y|w)$ is estimated by the *acoustic model*. Here we are using HMM as an acoustic model. Next we address the problem of how to estimate $P(y|w)$.

The *forward algorithm* can be used to compute the probability that a given model generated an observation sequence.

$$\alpha_i(t) = \begin{cases} 0 & t = 0 \ \& \ i \neq S_I \\ 1 & t = 0 \ \& \ i = S_I \\ \sum_j \alpha_j(t-1)a_{ji}b_{ji}(y_t) & t > 0 \end{cases}$$

$\alpha_i(t)$ is the probability that the Markov process is in state i having generated the sequence $y_1, y_2, \ldots, y_T$. The final probability for the model is given by $\alpha_{S_F}(T)$.

The trellis diagram in Figure 11.2 shows all possible state sequences. Each circle includes the cumulative probability at a particular state and time.

A slightly modified version of the forward algorithm is known as the *Viterbi algorithm*.

$$\alpha_i(t) = \begin{cases} 0 & t = 0 \;\&\; i \neq S_I \\ 1 & t = 0 \;\&\; i = S_I \\ \max_j \alpha_j(t-1)a_{ji}b_{ji}(y_t) & t > 0 \end{cases}$$

In each recursion, if we remember the state that has the highest probability, we can obtain the most likely state sequence in the model that produced the observations.

11.2.3. Estimation of HMM Parameters

The parameters of the model (transition probabilities and output probabilities) can be estimated by the *forward-backward algorithm* given a collection of training data. The forward-backward algorithm is also known as the *Baum-Welch algorithm*. It is based on the *Maximum Likelihood Estimation*.

First, we define the *backward calculation* $\beta_i(t)$, which is a counterpart of the forward calculation $\alpha_i(t)$.

$$\beta_i(t) = \begin{cases} 0 & t = T \;\&\; i \neq S_F \\ 1 & t = T \;\&\; i = S_F \\ \sum_j a_{ij}b_{ij}(y_{t+1})\beta_j(t+1) & 0 \leq t < T \end{cases}$$

$\beta_i(t)$ is the probability that the Markov process is in state i, and will generate the sequence $y_{t+1}, y_{t+2}, \ldots, y_T$.

Now given some initial parameters of the model, we could re-estimate them using the following iterative calculations.

$$\bar{a}_{ij} = \frac{\displaystyle\sum_{t=1}^{T} \alpha_i(t-1)a_{ij}b_{ij}(y_t)\beta_j(t)}{\displaystyle\sum_{t=1}^{T}\sum_{k} \alpha_i(t-1)a_{ik}b_{ik}(y_t)\beta_k(t)}$$

$$\bar{b}_{ij}(k) = \frac{\displaystyle\sum_{t:y_t=k} \alpha_i(t-1)a_{ij}b_{ij}(y_t)\beta_j(t)}{\displaystyle\sum_{t=1}^{T} \alpha_i(t-1)a_{ij}b_{ij}(y_t)\beta_j(t)}$$

The forward-backward algorithm has been proven to converge [1].

(1)	S	→	NP	VP
(2)	NP	→	DET	N
(3)	VP	→	V	
(4)	VP	→	V	NP
(5)	DET	→	/z/	/a/
(6)	DET	→	/z/	/i/
(7)	N	→	/m/ /ae/ /n/	
(8)	N	→	/ae/ /p/ /a/ /l/	
(9)	V	→	/iy/	/ts/
(10)	V	→	/s/ /ih/ /ng/ /s/	

Figure 11.3. An example of a grammar with phonetic lexicon.

11.3. HMM-LR Method

11.3.1. Basic Mechanism

This subsection gives an informal description of the HMM-LR method. We assume here that the HMM unit is the phone, although HMM can be used to represent any unit of speech, for example, word-based HMM, syllable-based HMM and phone-based HMM, etc.

In standard LR parsing, the next parser action (*shift*, *reduce*, *accept* or *error*) is determined using the current parser state and next input symbol to check the LR parsing table. This parsing mechanism is valid only for symbolic data and cannot be applied simply to continuous data such as speech.

In HMM-LR, the LR parser is used as a language source model for word/phone prediction/generation. Thus, we will hereafter call the LR parser the *predictive LR parser*. A phone-based predictive LR parser predicts next phones at each generation step and generates many possible sentences as phone sequences. The predictive LR parser determines next phones using the LR parsing table of the specified grammar and splits the parsing stack not only for grammatical ambiguity but also for phone variation. Because the predictive LR parser uses context-free rules whose terminal symbols are phone names, the phonetic lexicon for the specified task is embedded in the grammar. An example of context-free grammar rules with a phonetic lexicon is shown in Figure 11.3. Rule (5) indicates the definite article "the" before consonants, while rule (6) indicates the "the" before vowels. Rules (7), (8), (9) and (10) indicate the words "man", "apple", "eats" and "sings", respectively.

The HMM-LR continuous speech recognition system (see Figure 11.4) consists of the predictive LR parser and HMM phone verifiers. First, the parser picks up all phones predicted by the initial state of the LR parsing table and invokes the HMM models to verify the existence of these predicted phones. The parser then proceeds to the next state in the LR parsing table. During this process, all possible partial parses are constructed in parallel. The HMM phone verifier receives a *probability array* (see Figure 11.5) which includes end point

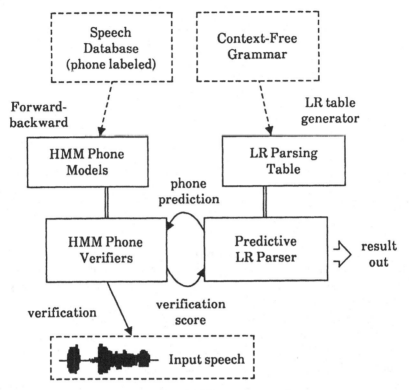

Figure 11.4. Schematic diagram of HMM-LR speech recognizer.

candidates and their probabilities, and updates it using an HMM probability calculation. This probability array is attached to each partial parse. When the highest probability in the array is under a certain threshold level, the partial parse is pruned. The parsing process proceeds in this way, and stops if the parser detects an accept action in the LR parsing table. In this case, if the best probability point reaches the end of the speech data, parsing ends successfully.

Very accurate, efficient speech parsing is achieved through the integrated processes of speech recognition and language analysis.

11.3.2. Algorithm

This subsection gives the algorithm for HMM-LR as a recognizer, which produces no parse trees. It is, however, easy to extend the algorithm to produce parse trees.

First, we introduce a data structure called a *cell*. A cell is a structure with information about one recognition candidate. The following are kept in the cell.

- *LR parsing stack*, with information for parsing control.
- *Probability array*, which includes end point candidates and their probabilities.

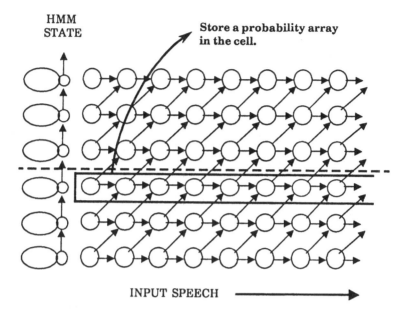

Figure 11.5. Stacking of a probability array

The algorithm is summarized below.

1. *Initialization.* Create a new cell C. Push the LR initial state 0 on top of the LR parsing stack of C. Initialize the probability array Q of C;

$$Q(t) = \begin{cases} 1 & t = 0 \\ 0 & 1 \leq t \leq T \end{cases}$$

2. *Ramification of cells.* Construct a set

$$S = \{(C, s, a, x) | \exists C, s, a, x \ (C \text{ is a cell which is not accepted}$$
$$\& \ s \text{ is the state on top of the LR parsing stack of } C$$
$$\& \ x = ACTION[s, a] \ \& \ x \neq \text{``error''}\})$$

For each element $(C, s, a, x) \in S$, do operations below. If a set S is empty, parsing is completed.

3. If $x = $ "*shift s'*", verify the existence of phone a. In this case, update the probability array Q of the cell C using the following computation.

$$\alpha_i(t) = \begin{cases} Q(t) & i = S_I \\ 0 & i \neq S_I \ \& \ t = 0 \\ \sum_j \alpha_j(t-1) a_{ji} b_{ji}(y_t) & i \neq 0 \ \& \ t > 0 \end{cases}$$

$$Q(t) = \begin{cases} 0 & t = 0 \\ \alpha_{S_F}(t) & t > 0 \end{cases}$$

If $\max_{1 \leq t \leq T} Q(t)$ is below a certain threshold, cell C is abandoned. Else push s' on top of the LR parsing stack of cell C.

4. If x = "*reduce $A \rightarrow \beta$*", pop $|\beta|$ symbols off the LR parsing stack and push $GOTO[s', A]$ where s' is the current state on top of the stack.
5. If x = "*accept*" and $Q(T)$ exceeds a certain threshold, cell C is accepted. If not, cell C is abandoned.
6. Return to 2.

Recognition results are kept in accepted cells. Generally, many recognition candidates exist, and it is possible to rank these candidates using a value $Q(T)$ of each cell.

11.3.3. Refinements of the Algorithm

The algorithm described above is a simple one. It is possible to make some refinements to the algorithm.

1. Using the beam-search technique.
   The *beam-search* technique was first used in the HARPY speech recognition system [12]. It is a modification of the breadth-first search technique, in which a group of near-miss alternatives around the best path are selected and processed in parallel. The beam-search technique reduces search cost and maintains search efficiency. Generally, a set S constructed in step 2 in the algorithm is quite large. The beam-search technique can be used to select a group of likely cells. The value $\max_{1 \leq t \leq T} Q(t)$ of each cell can be used as an evaluation score.
2. Using the graph-structured stack.
   The *graph-structured stack* is one of the key ideas in Generalized LR parsing. In the above algorithm, when making a set S, copies of an LR parsing stack are created. By using the graph-structured stack, it is not necessary to copy the whole stack. Copying only the necessary portion of the stack is sufficient. Thus, the amount of computation is reduced.

11.4. Case Study

In this section, we describe the implementation of a continuous speech recognition system based on HMM-LR method, developed at *ATR Interpreting Telephony Research Laboratories* [3]. This system recognizes Japanese phrase-wise utterances, and is used as the frond-end of the *SL-TRANS*, a spoken language translation system from Japanese into English [14].

11.4.1. Signal Processing

The speech is sampled at 12 KHz, pre-emphasized with a filter whose transform function is $(1 - 0.97z^{-1})$, and windowed using a 256-point Hamming window every 9 msec. Then, 12-order LPC analysis is carried out. Spectrum, difference cepstrum coefficients, and power are computed. Multiple VQ codebooks for each feature were generated using 216 phonetically balanced words.

Table 11.1. *Grammar complexity*

Vocabulary:	1,035 words
Task Entropy:	17.0
Phone Perplexity:	5.9
Estimated Word Perplexity:	more than 100

11.4.2. HMM Phone Models

A three-loop model for consonants and a one-loop model for vowels are trained using each phone data extracted from the ATR isolated word database [7].

To represent phone models with less distortion, separate vector quantization (multiple codebooks) are used, where spectrum, LPC cepstral difference and power are quantized separately. In the training stage the output vector probabilities of these three codebooks are estimated simultaneously and independently, and in the recognition stage all the output probabilities are calculated as the product of the output vector probabilities in these codebooks.

HMM is effective in expressing speech data statistically, but phone duration information from speech data is not modeled statistically in the HMM phone models. In order to make a statistical duration model, an HMM state duration control is realized as a state duration penalty calculated from an HMM state duration distribution of the training data.

As described above, HMM phone models were trained using the word utterances, whereas the recognition is carried out for continuous speech. To realize accurate duration control, HMM duration parameters were modified according to the speaking rates of word and phrase utterances.

11.4.3. Grammar

The grammar is designed to cover many linguistic phenomena common in Japanese. The complexity of the grammar is measured by *task entropy* and *phone perplexity* [4]. Task entropy is defined as average information obtained when an utterance is recognized correctly. The phone perplexity is defined as the average number of phones predicted at each step. The complexity of the grammar is summarized in Table 11.1.

There are 1,461 grammar rules including 1,035 different word, and the phone perplexity is 5.9. Assuming that the average phone length per word is three, the word perplexity will exceed 100.

11.4.4. Performance

The system was tested for four speakers (three male, one female) both in the speaker-dependent condition and in the speaker-adapted condition.

Table 11.2. *Recognition performance*

	Recognition Rate (%)	
Rank	Speaker Dependent	Speaker Adapted
1	89.5	80.2
2	96.4	93.1
3	98.6	95.8
4	99.0	97.4
5	99.3	98.1

The result is shown in Table 11.2. Average phrase recognition rate is 89.5%, and a rate of 99.3% is achieved for the top five choices in the speaker-dependent condition. In the speaker-adapted condition, rates are 80.2% and 98.1%, respectively.

11.5. Concluding Remarks

In this chapter, we have described HMM-LR, an accurate and efficient speech recognition/parsing method. We have also introduced a speech recognizer based on this method.

In HMM-LR, Generalized LR parsing is used as a language source model for word/phoneme prediction/generation. This characteristic of Generalized LR parsing can be applied to other approaches of speech recognition. Indeed, Generalized LR parsing is successfully integrated with *Time-Delay Neural Networks* [18] and attains good performance [13].

We have not considered the stochastic language modeling so far. From the viewpoint of information theory, every language has its own information entropy which includes probabilities of word occurrences and probabilities of word sequences. For example, N-gram language models (bigram, trigram, etc.) are extensively used to correct recognition errors and improve recognition accuracy [8,17] An N-gram language model is an extremely rough approximation of a language, but it is effective in correcting local syntax errors. Another approach to making a stochastic language model is to use a probabilistic context-free grammar [2] or a probabilistic LR parsing [19]. These stochastic language models can be incorporated into the HMM-LR speech recognizer, and attain better performance [6].

Acknowledgments

I would like to thank Dr. Akira Kurematsu, the president of ATR Interpreting Telephony Research Laboratories, for his encouragement and support. I would also like to thank Toshiyuki Hanazawa, Takeshi Kawabata, Kiyohiro Shikano,

Hiroaki Saito and Tsuyoshi Morimoto for their valuable technical suggestions and comments.

References

[1] Baum, L. E., Petrie, T., Soules, G., & Weiss, N., 1970, *A Maximization Technique Occurring in the Statistical Analysis of Probabilistic Functions of Markov Chains*, The Annals of Mathematical Statistics, Vol. 41.

[2] Fu, K. S., 1974, *Syntactic Methods in Pattern Recognition*, Academic Press.

[3] Hanazawa, T., Kita, K., Nakamura, S., Kawabata, T., & Shikano, K., 1990, *ATR HMM-LR Continuous Speech Recognition System*, Proc. of ICASSP 90 - IEEE International Conference on Acoustics, Speech and Signal Processing.

[4] Kawabata, T., Shikano, K., & Kita, K., 1989, *Task entropy and Phone Perplexity*, The Acoustic Society of Japan Spring Meeting Proc. (in Japanese).

[5] Kita, K., Kawabata, T., & Saito, H., 1989, *HMM Continuous Speech Recognition Using Predictive LR Parsing*, Proc. of ICASSP 89 - IEEE International Conference on Acoustics, Speech and Signal Processing.

[6] Kita, K., Kawabata, T., & Hanazawa, T., 1990, *HMM Continuous Speech Recognition Using Stochastic Language Models*, Proc. of ICASSP 90 - IEEE International Conference on Acoustics, Speech and Signal Processing.

[7] Kuwabara, H., Takeda, K., Sagisaka, Y., Katagiri, S., Morikawa, S., & Watanabe, T., 1989, *Construction of a Large-Scale Japanese Speech Database and its Management System*, Proc. of ICASSP 89 - IEEE International Conference on Acoustics, Speech and Signal Processing.

[8] Lee, K. F., Hon, H. W., & Reddy, R., 1990, *An Overview of the SPHINX Speech Recognition System*, IEEE Transactions on Acoustics, Speech, and Signal Processing, Vol. 38, No. 1.

[9] Levinson, S. E., Rabiner, L. R., & Sondhi, M. M., 1983, *An Introduction to the Application of the Theory of Probabilistic Functions of a Markov Process to Automatic Speech Recognition*, Bell Syst. Tech. J., Vol. 62, No. 4.

[10] Linde, Y., Buzo, A., & Gray, R. M., 1980, *An Algorithm for Vector Quantizer Design*, IEEE Transaction on Communications, COM-28.

[11] Lippmann, R. P., 1989, *Review of Neural Networks for Speech Recognition*, Neural Computation, Vol. 1, No. 1.

[12] Lowerre, B. & Reddy, R., 1980, *The HARPY Speech Recognition System*, in Trends in Speech Recognition, ed. Lea, W. A., Prentice-Hall.

[13] Minami, Y., Sawai, H., Miyatake, M., & Shikano, K., 1990, *Large Vocabulary Spoken Word Recognition Using Time-Delay Neural Network Phoneme Spotting and Predictive LR-Parsing*, Trans. Tech. Group Speech Acoust. Soc. Japan, SP89-99 (in Japanese).

[14] Morimoto, T., Ogura, K., Kita, K., Kogure, K., & Kakigahara, K., 1989, *Spoken Language Processing in SL-TRANS*, ATR Symposium on Basic Research for Telephone Interpretation.

[15] Poritz, A. B., 1988, *Hidden Markov Models: A Guided Tour*, Proc. of ICASSP 88 - IEEE International Conference on Acoustics, Speech and Signal Processing.

[16] Rabiner, L. R., Juang, B. H., 1986, *An Introduction to Hidden Markov Models*, IEEE ASSP Magazine.

[17] Shikano, K., 1987, *Improvement of Word Recognition Results by Trigram Model*, Proc. of ICASSP 87 - IEEE International Conference on Acoustics, Speech and Signal Processing.

[18] Waibel, A., Hanazawa, T., Hinton, G., Shikano, K., & Lang, K. J., 1989, *Phoneme Recognition Using Time-Delay Neural Networks*, IEEE Transactions on Acoustics, Speech, and Signal Processing, Vol. 37, No. 3.

[19] Wright, J. H. & Wrigley, E. N., 1988, *Linguistic Control in Speech Recognition*, Proc. 7th FASE Symposium.

[20] Zue, V., Glass, J., Phillips, M., & Seneff, S., 1989, *Acoustic Segmentation and Phonetic Classification in the SUMMIT System*, Proc. of ICASSP 89 - IEEE International Conference on Acoustics, Speech and Signal Processing.

Index

9 780792 392019